KT-458-363

Scenes and Stages

Edited by John O'Connor

HAMMERSMITH AND WEST
LONDON COLLEGE
LEARNING ⸱ ⸱ ⸱

DAW L263589 £6.50

Published by Heinemann Educational Publishers
Halley Court, Jordan Hill, Oxford OX2 8EJ
A division of Reed Educational and Professional Publishing Ltd

OXFORD MELBOURNE AUCKLAND
JOHANNESBURG BLANTYRE GABORONE
IBADAN PORTSMOUTH (NH) USA CHICAGO

IIII 2001

© Selection, introduction and activities, John O'Connor, 2001

All rights reserved. No part of this publication may be reproduced in any material form (including photocopying or storing it in any medium by electronic means and whether or not transiently or incidentally to some other use of this publication) without the prior written permission of the copyright owner, except in accordance with the provisions of the Copyright, Designs and Patents Act 1988 or under the terms of a licence issued by the Copyright Licensing Agency Ltd, 90 Tottenham Court Road, London W1P 0LP. Applications for the copyright owner's written permission to reproduce any part of this publication should be addressed in the first instance to the publisher.

05 04 03 02 01
10 9 8 7 6 5 4 3 2 1
ISBN 0 435 23331 9

Acknowledgements

The publishers gratefully acknowledge the following for permission to reproduce copyright material. Every effort has been made to trace copyright holders, but in some cases has proved impossible. The publishers would be happy to hear from any copyright holder that has not been acknowledged.

Extract from *Maid Marian and her Merry Men* by Tony Robinson © Tony Robinson, 1989. Reproduced with permission of BBC Worldwide Limited. Extract from *The Dumb Waiter* by Harold Pinter, published by Faber and Faber Limited. Reprinted with permission of the publishers. Extract from *The Revenger's Comedies* by Alan Ayckbourn, published by Faber and Faber Limited. Reprinted with permission of the publishers. Extract from *The Oresteian Trilogy* by Aeschylus, translated by Philip Vellacott (Penguin Classics 1956) Philip Vellacott, 1956. Reprinted with permission of Penguin Books. Extract from *Blackadder Goes Forth* by Richard Curtis and Ben Elton in *Blackadder: The Whole Damn Dynasty* (Michael Joseph 1988) © Richard Curtis and Ben Elton 1987. Reprinted with permission of Penguin Books. Extract from *Loot* by Joe Orton, published by Methuen. Reprinted with permission of Methuen Publishing Limited. Extract from *Tales From Ovid* by Ted Hughes, adapted by Tim Supple and Simon Reade, published by Faber and Faber Limited. Reprinted with permission of the publishers. Extract from *Shakespeare in Love* screenplay by Tom Stoppard and Marc Norman, published by Faber and Faber Limited. Reprinted with permission of the publishers. Extract from *The Mysteries* by Tony Harrison, published by Faber and Faber Limited. Reprinted with permission of the publishers. Extract from *Waiting for Godot* by Samuel Becket, published by Faber and Faber Limited. Reprinted with permission of the publishers. Extract from *Educating Rita* by Willy Russell, published by Methuen. Reprinted with permission of Methuen Publishing Limited. Extract from *The Complete Fawlty Towers* by John Cleese and Connie Booth, published by Methuen 1989. Reprinted with permission of Methuen Publishing Limited. Extract from *Pygmalion* by George Bernard Shaw. Reprinted with permission of The Society of Authors on behalf of the Bernard Shaw Estate. Extract from *Our Country's Good* by Timberlake Wertenbaker, published by Methuen 1996. Reprinted with permission of Methuen Publishing Limited. Extract from *Journey's End* by R. C. Sherriff © R.C. Sherriff, 1929. Reproduced with permission of Curtis Brown Group Limited, London on behalf of the Estate of R.C. Sherriff. Extract from *Doctor Faustus* by Christopher Marlowe, edited by John D. Jump, published by Methuen 1970. Reprinted with permission of Methuen Publishing Limited. Extract from *An Inspector Calls* by J. B. Priestley © J. B. Priestley 1947. Reprinted by permission of Peters Fraser & Dunlop on behalf of the Estate of J. B. Priestley. Extract from *I Will Marry When I Want* by Ngugi wa Thiong'o and Ngugi wa Mirii, published by Heinemann. Reprinted with permission of REPP. Extract from *Statements* by Athol Fugard, John Kani, Winston Ntshona, published by OUP 1974 . . . Extract from *Top Girls* by Caryl Churchill, published by Methuen 1988. Reprinted with permission of Methuen Publishing Limited. Extract from *The Odyssey* version by Derek Walcott, published by Faber and Faber Limited in 1933. Reprinted by permission of Faber and Faber Limited. Extract from *Sherlock Holmes and The Limehouse Horror* by Philip Pullman. Reprinted with permission of A. P. Watt Limited on behalf of Philip Pullman. Extract from *The Woman in Black* adapted by Stephen Mallatratt from the book by Susan Hill. Original novel *The Woman in Black* © 1983 by Susan Hill. Adaptation 1989 by Susan Hill/Stephen Mallatratt. First published by Samuel French 1989. Reproduced by permission of The Agency (London) Limited. All rights reserved and enquiries to The Agency (London) Limited, 24 Pottery Lane, London W11 4LZ. Fax: 0207 727 9037.

The Publishers have made every effort to trace the copyright holders, but if they have inadvertently overlooked any, they will be pleased to make the necessary arrangements at the first opportunity.

Cover design by Miller Craig and Cocking
Cover photograph from 'The Performing Arts Library'
Typeset by 🞄 Tek-Art, Croydon, Surrey
Printed and bound in the United Kingdom by Clays Ltd, St Ives plc

Tel: 01865 888058 www.heinemann.co.uk

309528

Contents

Section D: Viewpoints on Society

Section E: Myth and Morality

Section F: Mystery and Suspense

Introduction for teachers

The texts

The extracts which make up *Scenes and Stages* have been put together with the aim of providing an introduction to English drama for students at Key Stage 3. Many of the authors (such as Shakespeare, Marlowe and Pinter) are recommended in the National Curriculum; others (including Tony Robinson, Grant and Naylor, Richard Curtis and Ben Elton) have been selected because they offer high-quality and entertaining scripts which are immediately accessible to young people.

The plays featured are arranged according to genre. Within each genre section, the extracts have been chosen to represent drama from several different centuries and, in many cases, from a variety of traditions.

Any collection which sets out to introduce young readers to drama from earlier centuries, or even a wide range of modern plays, will inevitably include some challenging texts: authors such as Samuel Beckett are not traditionally part of the Key Stage 3 diet. In these cases, extracts have been found which are not only representative of the writer and genre, but also comparatively accessible. Throughout the collection, these more challenging texts have been balanced by ones which are much more straightforward, but equally fruitful. In each section, the more accessible texts come first.

The activities

Each extract has a brief introduction, establishing the context, and is accompanied by three activities. These are all intended to support the text level objectives in the Framework for teaching English, and focus on Speaking and Listening, Reading and Writing.

The arrangement of extracts, followed by activities that help meet specific objectives in the Framework can be used to suit the lesson structure suggested in the Framework:

1 Short lesson starter (using the introduction to the extract)
2 Introduce the main teaching points (based upon the NLS references after each activity)
3 Develop the main teaching points (through individual or group work on the activities)
4 Plenary to draw out the learning (through feedback and presentation).

The practice of Guided Reading and Guided Writing, as outlined in the Framework, is one way in which to enable students in groups to work intensively on the objectives focused upon in the activities.

The National Curriculum requirements and Framework objectives addressed throughout he collection are detailed at the back of this book, together with a timeline and key to the extracts.

John O'Connor

Section A: Comedy

Comedy can take many forms, and audiences laugh at many different things – from Blackadder's witty insults to the practical joke played upon Malvolio in *Twelfth Night*. But, from its earliest days in ancient Greece, comedy has always been concerned with the things that make human beings ridiculous, as this collection of extracts shows.

Of course, we don't all laugh at the same things: a hugely successful television comedy will be totally unfunny to some people. But the interesting thing is how little the ingredients of comedy have changed over the centuries. For example, audiences in ancient Rome loved to see clever plots involving comic servants; and we are still enjoying these elements today, with Baldrick in *Blackadder* or Manuel in *Fawlty Towers*.

Many comedies through the ages have involved deception: cunning people tricking dim ones, or servants fooling their masters and mistresses; while one of the richest sources of laughter has been the language itself, and the ways in which people such as Mrs Malaprop or Manuel have wrestled with it – and lost. Both of these strands – deception and the English language – are highlighted in the selection which follows.

A1: Maid Marian and Her Merry Men

Writer: Tony Robinson
Date: 1989
Staging: Any acting space. The script used here is adapted from the original television script. This means that camera directions have been rewritten as speeches for the two narrators.
The story so far
The peasants in Worksop village are persecuted by the Sheriff of Nottingham and have nothing to eat but mud. At the end of the first scene, Barrington the minstrel reflects upon the harsh conditions under which the villagers live and wonders who will come to rescue them.

BARRINGTON   But even though they're poor and sore
The people have a dream
One day someone will come along
Who'll turn their mud to cream
Someone who'll fight for the people's rights
And set all the people free
Who'll whip the Sheriff and Bad King John
But who will this someone be?

NARRATOR 1   Marian enters

MARIAN   I think he means me.
With my ruthless band of freedom fighters.

Trumpet flourish.

BARRINGTON   Now who will this someone be?

Scene 2 Worksop village

Narrators 1 and 2, Sheriff, Rabies and Gary.

NARRATOR 2 The Sheriff comes out of a tumbledown hut with a boutique sign on it.

SHERIFF And when you've finished them, sew on the Royal Coat of Arms.

RABIES Excuse me, my Lord. *(Holding out a hand for money.)*

SHERIFF *(calling into the hut)* I'll be back in ten minutes, so make sure they're ready.

RABIES My Lord?

SHERIFF Go away!

RABIES Remember me, my Lord?

SHERIFF No, I never met you before in my life. If I had, I'd have chopped your face off for polluting the environment.

RABIES But what about my raffle?

SHERIFF What raffle?

RABIES The raffle what you took all the tickets for.

SHERIFF You're running a raffle?

RABIES Yes.

SHERIFF Then where's your licence?

RABIES What licence?

SHERIFF Guards!

NARRATOR 1 Enter Gary and Graeme, two very large and very dim Norman guards.

GARY Hullo!

SHERIFF *(to guards)* I'm arresting this man for being in possession of a raffle without a licence. And I'm confiscating all his prizes. This village needs cleaning up! *(Aside)* And what's more, Mrs Nottingham and I could do with a nice holiday for two.

Scene 3 In front of a peasant's hut

Narrators 1 and 2, Barrington, Old Lady and Sheriff.

NARRATOR 2 An old lady peasant is sitting in front of some muddy washing.

BARRINGTON *(furtively)* Hey Gladys man, you hungry?

OLD LADY Barrington, I'm always hungry.

BARRINGTON D'you wanna buy some rats?

OLD LADY *(she becomes equally furtive)* Rats! Wicked! Let's have a look.

NARRATOR 2 Barrington opens his coat to reveal several rows of rats of all sizes pinned to the inside.

BARRINGTON What flavour d'you want? I've got cheese and onion, salt and vinegar, prawn cocktail. And this little fellow's new on the market – barbequed chicken with cream cheese and chives.

NARRATOR 1 The Sheriff bursts on to the scene from behind the washing.

SHERIFF Got you, sunshine! You are nicked!

BARRINGTON What do you mean, man. I haven't done nuffink.

SHERIFF There is a 'sell-by' date stamped on the bottom of that rat; what's it say, Barrington?

BARRINGTON *(reads)* 16th July, 1195.

SHERIFF And what's today, Barrington?

BARRINGTON 17th July, 1195.

SHERIFF So you're selling foul, stinking, rotten mouldy goods to innocent little old ladies, aren't you, son? It's the stocks for you, my lad! Followed by a nice little trial up at Nottingham Castle. Guards!

NARRATOR 2 Barrington is dragged away to join Rabies in the stocks. The peasants look on, silently disapproving.

A2: The Revengers' Comedies

Writer: Alan Ayckbourn
Date: 1989
Staging: This play was written for the Theatre-in-the-round at
Scarborough. The opening scene needs a set which represents the
pathway over a London bridge. The stage directions also call for
'perhaps a little mist' and the sounds of distant traffic and a
ship's siren.
The story so far
This is the opening of the play.

ACT I

Prologue

> *Midnight. Albert Bridge, SW3. Perhaps a little river mist.*
> *Distant traffic, a ship's siren, Henry, a man in his early forties,*
> *appears in a pool of street light on the bridge. He is wrapped*
> *in an overcoat and scarf. He is hunched and miserable. He*
> *stares over the edge, deciding whether to jump. From his*
> *expression, it's evidently a long way down. He says a little*
> *silent prayer, as though asking forgiveness, and makes to*
> *climb over the railing. He is uncomfortably straddled across*
> *the railing and in some discomfort when he hears a woman's*
> *voice from the darkness.*

KAREN   *(calling)* Help . . . Help . . . Please help me . . .

> *Henry stops and listens, rather startled.*

Please help . . . somebody . . .

HENRY   *(calling, tentatively)* Hallo?

KAREN   *(calling back)* Hallo . . .

HENRY   *(calling again)* Hallo?

KAREN Would you stop saying hallo and come and help me, please? I've got myself caught up here . . .

HENRY Oh, right. Hang on, there . . . Just hang on . . .

He starts to clamber back on to the bridge.

KAREN I don't have any option. I've been hanging here for hours.

HENRY Just one very small second . . .

Henry moves to the source of her voice. As he does so, we make out Karen for the first time. She is in her mid-twenties. She wears a woolly hat and a lightweight coat over an evening dress. She is hanging outside the bridge railing. All that seems to be keeping her from falling is the belt of her coat, which has become entangled with the ironwork. Henry reaches her.

Oh, Lord. How can I . . . ?

KAREN *(trying to indicate)* Do you see? Something's caught – I think it's the belt of my coat . . .

HENRY Oh, yes, yes. Look, I think I'd better . . . *(Flustered)* Look – er . . . Yes, yes. I think I'd better try and – er . . . Would you mind if I – tried to lift you . . .?

KAREN You can do what you like – just get me off this bloody bridge . . .

HENRY Yes, yes, right . . .

He studies the problem.

KAREN Can you see? I think it's my belt . . .

HENRY Yes, yes, so it is. I think I'd better get that free before I . . .

He starts to untangle the belt.

KAREN Careful . . .

HENRY Yes. Only I don't want to tear your coat, you see. If I tried to lift you over as you are, I might damage it . . . It's a very nice coat . . .

KAREN	(sarcastically) Well, that's very considerate of you . . . Thank you.
HENRY	(finally freeing the belt) Right. There you go, all free.
KAREN	Aaaarh!

The sudden release of the belt all but causes her to lose her balance and topple over the edge. She grabs at the first available handhold, which happens to be Henry's scarf.

HENRY	(choking) Hurrgh!
KAREN	(screaming) Hold on to me, for God's sake!
HENRY	(with difficulty) Hould hoo hossibly het ho hof hy harf? Hi han't –
KAREN	Don't let go . . .
HENRY	Hi han't . . .
KAREN	What?
HENRY	Hi han't heathe . . .
KAREN	Well, give me something else to hold. (Angrily) Quickly, you're so useless . . . You're so totally, totally useless . . . What are you doing on this bridge, anyway?

Henry manages to put his arms under hers and around her middle. Karen releases his scarf.

HENRY	(Much relieved) Ah! Thank you. OK, I'm going to try and pull you over. Ready?
KAREN	Right.
HENRY	And – heave . . .

Henry hauls at her. Karen reacts.

KAREN	Aaargh! Careful!
HENRY	Sorry. It's a question of leverage . . .
KAREN	Well, could you use another bit of me to lever with?

HENRY	Yes, I'm sorry, I didn't mean to . . . *(He finds another grip.)* That better?
KAREN	Fractionally. Those are only my ribs.
HENRY	And two–six! Hup!

He starts to heave her over.

KAREN	*(reacting)* Hah!
HENRY	*(another heave)* Hip!
KAREN	Hoo!
HENRY	Sorry, is this hurting?
KAREN	No, it's quite nice, actually. Keep going.
HENRY	*(a final heave)* Hoy!
KAREN	Huf!

He finally half lifts, half drags her over the railing. Karen finishes sitting on the bridge. Henry regains his breath.

God! That was terrifying.

HENRY	Close thing.
KAREN	It certainly was. *(She shudders. She looks around her as if searching for someone.)*
HENRY	You all right?
KAREN	Thank you very much.
HENRY	Not at all.
KAREN	You saved my life.
HENRY	Well . . .
KAREN	I must owe you something . . . ?
HENRY	No.
KAREN	Something. A drink, at least?
HENRY	*(looking at his watch)* It's half-past twelve.
KAREN	Half-past twelve?

HENRY	Yes.
KAREN	*(angrily)* My God! Half-past *twelve?*
HENRY	Yes.
KAREN	I don't believe it.
HENRY	How long had you been there?
KAREN	Since twenty past eight.
HENRY	Lord.
KAREN	Half-past twelve! It's unbelievable.

Pause.

HENRY	Well . . .
KAREN	This is Chelsea Bridge, isn't it?
HENRY	No, this is Albert Bridge.
KAREN	Albert Bridge?
HENRY	Yes.
KAREN	You sure?
HENRY	Positive.
KAREN	Sod it!
HENRY	What?
KAREN	Nothing.

Another pause.

HENRY	Er . . . How did you come to get there?
KAREN	Where?
HENRY	Where you were. Hanging like that? How did you get there? Do you mind my asking?
KAREN	Well, obviously, I was trying to throw myself off.
HENRY	*You* were?
KAREN	Only I managed to make a complete mess of that, too. Like everything else in my life . . . *(Suddenly despairing)* Oh, God . . .

She hunches up, tearfully, a pathetic huddle on the pavement.

HENRY   *(ineffectually)* Oh, come on, now . . .

KAREN   You can leave me, it's all right. Leave me here. I'm just so pathetic . . .

HENRY   Look, perhaps I could see you home . . .?

KAREN   Go away. Just leave me here . . .

HENRY   I can't do that.

KAREN   I'll be all right. I expect.

HENRY   I can't leave you here like this.

KAREN   *(a little cry of self-pity)* Oh . . .

HENRY   *(soothingly)* Sssh!

KAREN   Oh!

HENRY   Please let me . . . at least get you on your feet. You'll catch your – you'll catch your cold sitting there.

Karen lets Henry help her to her feet.

There.

HENRY   *(holding on to him)* Thank you. You're very kind.

HENRY   *(slightly embarrassed)* No, not really. I just –

KAREN   I'm sorry I called you useless. I didn't mean that.

HENRY   No, as it happens you were right. I am a bit useless, really.

KAREN   Yes? Is that how you see yourself? Useless?

HENRY   Most of the time.

KAREN   Well. That makes two of us, then, doesn't it?

She smiles a little.

HENRY   *(smiling too, despite himself)* I suppose it does.

Karen evidently decides to pull herself together. She scrabbles in her mac pocket and eventually finds a tissue.

KAREN Come on . . .

HENRY *(startled)* Where to?

KAREN I'll take you somewhere for a drink. Come on.

HENRY But nothing will be open.

KAREN I know somewhere that's open. It's all right, it's not far . . . Do you have your car with you?

HENRY I don't have one.

KAREN Mine's parked along there . . . Come on, we both need something. Unless you've other things you'd sooner be doing?

HENRY *(looking back at the river)* Er, no. No.

KAREN Great. *(Turning and extending her hand)* By the way. Karen. Karen Knightly.

HENRY *(shaking her hand in turn)* Henry. Henry Bell.

KAREN Splendid. Then follow me, Henry Bell.

HENRY Where are we going?

KAREN *(disappearing into the darkness)* Just as far as the bypass, that's all . . .

HENRY Ah. *(As he follows her off, puzzled)* What bypass?

The lights dim and almost immediately return to reveal –

A3: Twelfth Night

Writer: William Shakespeare
Date: 1601 or 1602
Staging: We don't know where *Twelfth Night* was first acted; but there were certainly performances in the Globe playhouse. It was also performed in one of the Inns of Court (colleges for lawyers) in London.

The story so far

Lady Olivia inhabits a grand house. Living with her are her uncle, Sir Toby Belch, a jester called Feste, the housekeeper Maria, a gentleman called Fabian and the steward (a man who looks after the running of the house) called Malvolio. Sir Toby has also invited a rich companion to stay – Sir Andrew Aguecheek – in the hopes of marrying him off to his niece. When Malvolio spoils their nightly drinking sessions and threatens to cause trouble, Maria devises a plot to make him look ridiculous. She writes a letter in Olivia's handwriting which makes Malvolio believe that his mistress is in love with him. Not only that, but the letter encourages him to approach Olivia wearing yellow stockings and smiling.

ACT III

Scene 4

> *Olivia's Garden. Enter Olivia and Maria.*

OLIVIA   *(aside)* I have sent after him; he says he'll come.
How shall I feast him? What bestow of him?
For youth is bought more oft than begged or
   borrowed.

I speak too loud.

(To Maria) Where is Malvolio? He is **sad and civil**,

How shall I feast him? How shall I entertain him? What shall I give him?
sad and civil serious and dignified.

And suits well for a servant with my fortunes.
Where's Malvolio?

MARIA   He's coming, madam; but in very strange manner.
He is sure **possessed**, madam.

OLIVIA   Why, what's the matter? Does he rave?   10

MARIA   No, madam, he does nothing but smile. Your ladyship
were best to have some guard about you if he come;
for sure the man is **tainted in's wits**.

OLIVIA   Go call him **hither** *(Exit Maria.)* I am as mad as he,
If sad and merry madness equal be.

Enter Maria with Malvolio.

How now; Malvolio?

MALVOLIO   Sweet lady, ho, ho.

OLIVIA   Smil'st thou? I sent for thee upon a sad occasion.

MALVOLIO   Sad, lady! I could be sad. This does make some
obstruction in the blood, this **cross-gartering**; but   20
what of that? If it please the eye of one, it is with me as
the very true sonnet is, 'Please one and please all'.

OLIVIA   Why, how dost thou, man? What is the matter with thee?

MALVOLIO   Not black in my mind, though yellow in my legs. It did
come to his hands, and commands shall be executed.
I think we do know the sweet **Roman hand**.

OLIVIA   Wilt thou go to bed, Malvolio?

MALVOLIO   To bed? Ay, sweet heart, and I'll come to thee.

OLIVIA   God comfort thee! Why dost thou smile so, and kiss
thy hand so oft?   30

----

possessed mad.
tainted in's wits disturbed in his mind.
hither here.
cross-gartering a way of tying garters around the leg, above and behind the knee.
Roman hand italic handwriting.

MARIA	How do you, Malvolio?
MALVOLIO	At your request? Yes, nightingales answer **daws**.
MARIA	Why appear you with this ridiculous boldness before my lady?
MALVOLIO	'Be not afraid of greatness.' 'Twas well writ.
OLIVIA	What meanest thou by that, Malvolio?
MALVOLIO	'Some are born great' –
OLIVIA	Ha?
MALVOLIO	'Some achieve greatness' –
OLIVIA	What sayest thou?
MALVOLIO	'And some have greatness thrust upon them.'
OLIVIA	Heaven **restore thee!**
MALVOLIO	'Remember who **commended** thy yellow stockings' –
OLIVIA	'Thy yellow stockings'?
MALVOLIO	'And wished to see thee cross-gartered.'
OLIVIA	'Cross-gartered'?
MALVOLIO	'Go to, thou art made, if thou desirest to be so' –
OLIVIA	Am I 'made'?
MALVOLIO	'If not, let me see thee a servant still.'
OLIVIA	Why, this is very midsummer madness.

Enter Servant.

SERVANT	Madam, the young gentleman of the Count Orsino's is returned. **I could hardly entreat him back**. He attends your ladyship's pleasure.

40

50

---

daws Jackdaws (common birds).
restore thee bring you back to sanity.
commended praised.
I could hardly entreat him back I had difficulty keeping him out.

OLIVIA I'll come to him *(Exit Servant.)* Good Maria, let this fellow be **looked to**. Where's my cousin Toby? Let some of my people have a special care of him; I would not have him **miscarry** for the half of my **dowry**.

Exeunt Olivia and Maria, severally.

MALVOLIO O, ho, **do you come near me** now? No worse man than Sir Toby to look to me? This concurs directly   60
with the letter: she sends him on purpose, that I may appear **stubborn** to him; for she **incites** me to that in the letter. '**Cast thy humble slough**', says she. 'Be opposite with a kinsman, surly with servants; let thy tongue **tang arguments of state; put thyself into the trick of singularity**'; and consequently sets down the manner how; as, a sad face, a **reverend carriage**, a **slow tongue, in the habit of some sir of note**, and so forth. I have **limed** her; but it is Jove's doing, and Jove make me thankful. And when she went away now,   70
'Let this fellow be looked to'. 'Fellow' not 'Malvolio', nor after my **degree**, but 'fellow'. Why, **every thing adheres together, that no dram of a scruple, no**

---

looked to taken care of.

miscarry come to harm.

dowry her future marriage settlement.

do you come near me . . . ? do you begin to understand me . . .?

stubborn rude.

incites encourages.

Cast thy humble slough Throw off your humility. (He is quoting lines from the letter she is supposed to have written.)

tang arguments of state speak out on serious subjects.

put thyself . . . singularity behave eccentrically.

reverend carriage dignified way of walking.

slow tongue thoughtful way of speaking.

in the habit . . . note in the dress and behaviour of an important person.

limed caught.

degree rank.

every thing adheres . . . scruple it all fits – there's not the tiniest doubt.

scruple of a scruple, no obstacle, **no incredulous or unsafe circumstance** – What can be said? Nothing that can be can come between me and the **full prospect** of my hopes. Well, **Jove**, not I, is the doer of this, and he is to be thanked.

Enter Maria with Sir Toby and Fabian.

SIR TOBY Which way is he, in the name of sanctity? If all the devils of hell be drawn in little, and **Legion** himself possessed him, yet I'll speak to him. 80

FABIAN Here he is, here he is. How is't with you, sir? How is't with you, man?

---

no incredulous ... circumstance nothing unbelievable or cannot be depended on.
full prospect total fulfilment.
Jove the Roman King of the gods.
Legion a character in the Bible who was possessed by many devils.

A4: Red Dwarf

Writers: Rob Grant and Doug Naylor
Date: 1993
Staging: Television. The terms 'Int.' and 'Ext.' stand for 'interior' (a scene which takes place indoors) and 'exterior' (outdoors).
The story so far
The crew of *Starbug* have crash-landed on a freezing cold planet. While Kryten (the robot) and the Cat (a mutated life-form) go off in search of help, Rimmer (a hologram) and Lister (a human) try to keep warm enough to stay alive.

The temperature drops and more objects go on the fire. So far they have burnt nearly everything they can find, including Rimmer's works of Shakespeare. The only things left seem to be Rimmer's savings and his collection of nineteenth-century model soldiers.

---

16 Model shot

> Starbug *in blizzard.*

17 Int. Starbug rear. Day

> *Shot: the stove. Money is burning. Another wad lands on top of it.*

RIMMER How much has gone so far?

LISTER Five thousand eight hundred.

RIMMER Five thousand eight hundred!

> *Lister throws on another wad.*

LISTER Six grand.

RIMMER The whole twenty-four grand isn't going to last an hour, is it? *(Nearly in tears)* It took me ten years to save that. Ten years!

LISTER	I'd better start unpacking the soldiers.
RIMMER	No. There must be something else to burn. There must be.
LISTER	There isn't. I've looked. Listen, I know it's a bummer. I know it must be heartbreaking. But it's only *stuff*. It's just possessions. In the end, they're not important. They might go for a bundle in some swanky Islington antique shop – but right here, and right now, all they are is nicely painted firewood.

Lister throws on some more money.

RIMMER	This isn't happening. It's a nightmare.
LISTER	You've got to get your priorities right. It's like those people you read about who run back into a burning house to rescue some treasured piece of furniture and wind up burning to death. Nothing is more important than a human life . . .

Rimmer is looking in the corner of the room.

RIMMER	What about your guitar?
LISTER	. . . Except my guitar.
RIMMER	Why didn't we think of it before? We can burn your guitar.
LISTER	Not my *guitar*, Rimmer.
RIMMER	It's made of wood.
LISTER	Yeah, but it's my guitar. I've had it since I was sixteen. It's an authentic Les Paul copy.
RIMMER	But it's not worth anything. It's just a thing. It's just a possession.
LISTER	Yes, but it's mine.
RIMMER	How is it any different from my soldiers?

LISTER   It's my lifeline. I . . . I need that guitar. When it gets to
          me – I mean the loneliness – when it gets on top of
          me . . . it's the only way I can escape. I mean, I know
          I'm not exactly a wizard on it, and it's only got five
          strings, and three of them are G, but the whole of my
          life I've never had anything to hang on to – no roots,
          no parents, no education . . .

RIMMER   No education?

LISTER   I went to art college. All I've ever had is that guitar. It's
          the only thing in the whole of my miserable smegging
          life that hasn't walked out on me. Don't make me
          burn it.

RIMMER   *(quietly)* We've got to.

          Lister hangs his head

LISTER   *(pause)* Look. This is going to sound pretty stupid . . .
          but I'd just like to play one more song on it. One for
          the road.

RIMMER   Sure, sure. I mean – I'm not enjoying this.

LISTER   I know, I, uh . . . Thanks, man.

          *Lister picks up the guitar, and walks off to a fairly dim corner.
          He strums a chord. Rimmer is looking at the floor, slightly
          embarrassed. In his most feeble, plaintive voice, Lister
          begins to sing:*

LISTER   *(singing)* 'She's out of my life . . . She's out of my life.'
          (Spoken) My step-dad taught me this one. First song
          I ever learned to play. *(Sings)* 'And I don't know
          whether to laugh or cry . . .'

          Rimmer gets up embarrassed.

RIMMER   I, uh, just, uh . . . *(Points at the door.)*

          He walks up to the door.

18 Ext. Crashed Starbug. Blizzard

Rimmer walks into the howling blizzard.

19 Int. Starbug rear. Day

Lister puts down the guitar and nips over to the door to check Rimmer's gone. Carrying the guitar, Lister nips over to the trunk, puts the guitar against the trunk, takes a pencil out of his top pocket and starts tracing the guitar shape on to the back of the trunk. He picks up a hacksaw.

20 Ext. Crashed Starbug. Blizzard

Rimmer looks at his watch, then back at the ship.

21 Int. Starbug rear. Day

By now Lister has removed a complete guitar shape out of the back of Rimmer's trunk. He pushes the trunk back against the wall, slips his guitar inside the green locker on the far wall, then crosses to the stove, and breaks the guitar-shaped piece of wood over his knee.

22 Ext. Crashed Starbug. Blizzard

Rimmer walking up to the door.

23 Int. Starbug rear. Day

The door opens and Rimmer comes in. Lister is sitting at the stove, guitar-shaped pieces of wood burning merrily away.

RIMMER	I don't know what to say.
LISTER	Nothing *to* say.
RIMMER	You've made a supreme sacrifice. You know that? A *supreme* sacrifice.
LISTER	Had to be done.
RIMMER	I've been judging the book by its cover, haven't I? All these years, that's what I've been doing. But when it really comes down to it, you're one heck of a regular guy.

Lister grunts.

RIMMER	There's no point being modest. I know what that guitar meant to you. The same as that trunk means to me. If that trunk got so much as scratched, I'd be devastated. It's not the outward value – for me, that trunk is a link to the past. A link to the father I never managed to square things with . . .
LISTER	*(slightly panicky)* Is it?
RIMMER	It's the only thing he ever gave me, apart from . . . apart from his disappointment.

Lister covers his face.

RIMMER	But you've shown me, by burning your guitar, what true value is.

Lister gives a low moan.

RIMMER	Decency. Self-sacrifice. Those are the things that make up real wealth. And from where I'm standing . . . I'm a pretty rich man.
LISTER	Oh, god.
RIMMER	Burn the soldiers.
LISTER	No. Not the soldiers too.
RIMMER	You burnt your guitar. I want to make a sacrifice, too. Burn the Armée du Nord. Cast them to the flames: let

them lay down their lives for the sake of friendship. *(Sniffs the air)* What's that smell?

LISTER What smell? I can't smell any smell.

RIMMER *(sniffs)* Camphor.

LISTER Oh, god.

RIMMER Your guitar was made of camphor wood! It was probably worth a fortune. Burn the soldiers – burn them right now.

24 Ext. Blizzard

We see two torches in the distance, coming towards us. Over, we hear:

KRYTEN I can't go on.

CAT You've got to go on, buddy: we're nearly there.

KRYTEN I've no strength.

CAT Come on, you can make it.

They come into view. Kryten is pulling the heavily laden sleigh, with the Cat sitting on it. Cat whips the air.

CAT Look – there they are. Mush! Mush!

25 Int. Starbug rear. Day

The soldiers are burning away. Rimmer is peering into the stove. After a while, he starts quietly imitating a trumpet, playing the 'Last Post' . Finally, he finishes.

RIMMER Au revoir, mes amis. A bientôt.

LISTER Look – there's something I've got to tell you . . . something awful.

RIMMER	If it's about how you finished off the dog food, Dave, I understand.
LISTER	No. It's not about that.

The door opens, and Kryten and the Cat enter.

CAT	Hey, hey, hey!
LISTER	Cat! Kryten! You made it – you found us!
RIMMER	So where've you been the last six days?
KRYTEN	We rendezvoused with Holly. Then, after two days, when you still hadn't turned up, I said we should go and look for you.
CAT	We have been everywhere. Fourteen moons, two planets. I've been so worried – I haven't buffed my shoes in two days.
RIMMER	So – Holly managed to navigate her way through five Black Holes?

Holly appears on Kryten's chest monitor.

HOLLY	As it transpired, there weren't any Black Holes.
RIMMER	But you saw them – you saw them on the monitor.
HOLLY	They weren't Black Holes.
RIMMER	What were they?
HOLLY	Grit. Five specks of grit on the scanner-scope. See, the thing about grit is, it's black, and the thing about scanner-scopes . . .
RIMMER	Oh, shut up.
LISTER	*(sighs)* Come on. Let's go.

Lister and the Cat go out.

| RIMMER | Something happened here, Kryten. Something that made us closer. I saw a side of Dave Lister that I didn't even know existed. He's not just an irresponsible, |

selfish drifter, out for number one. He's a man . . .
He's a Man of Honour.

Lister comes back in. Looking at the floor, he crosses to the locker.

LISTER Excuse me.

He opens the locker, takes out his guitar and exits. Rimmer looks at the door, then at the fire, then, slowly, he turns to his trunk.

RIMMER Open the trunk.

Kryten goes to open the trunk. We shoot through the guitar-shaped hole at the back of the trunk as the trunk opens, and Rimmer peers in.

A5: Loot

Writer: Joe Orton
Date: 1965
Staging: A set to represent an ordinary living room in an ordinary house.
The story so far
Hal and Dennis have stolen some money. It is just after the death of Hal's mother and her body, in its coffin, stands in the living-room. Dennis is screwing the lid down when Hal has an idea.

Hal stares at the coffin as Dennis screws the lid down.

HAL   Has anybody ever hidden money in a coffin?

Dennis looks up. Pause.

DENNIS   Not when it was in use.

HAL   Why not?

DENNIS   It's never crossed anybody's mind.

HAL   It's crossed mine.

He takes the screwdriver from Dennis, and begins to unscrew the coffin lid.

It's the comics I read. Sure of it.

DENNIS   *(wiping his forehead with the back of his hand)* Think of your mum. Your lovely old mum. She gave you birth.

HAL   I should thank anybody for that?

DENNIS   Cared for you. Washed your nappies. You'd be some kind of monster.

Hal takes the lid off the coffin.

HAL   Think what's at stake. *(He goes to the wardrobe and unlocks it.)* Money.

He brings out the money. Dennis picks up a bundle of notes, looks into the coffin.

DENNIS Won't she rot it? The body juices? I can't believe it's possible.

HAL She's embalmed. Good for centuries.

Dennis puts a bundle of notes into the coffin. Pause. He looks at Hal.

DENNIS There's no room.

Hal lifts the corpse's arm.

HAL *(pause, frowns)* Remove the corpse. Plenty of room then.

DENNIS Seems a shame really. The embalmers have done a lovely job.

A6: Mak the Sheep-stealer

Writers: Not known.
Date: The thirteenth century. This modern version is by Tony Harrison.
Staging: This episode is taken from one of a number of individual short plays which made up a mystery cycle. Mystery plays took their names from the 'mysteries' or craft guilds (from the French word *métier*, a craft) who staged them. A town such as Wakefield, where this play comes from, would put on a whole cycle of plays, based on stories from the Bible, which could last all day, or even longer. They were performed on mobile stages built on carts, called 'pageant wagons', which could be pulled around the town. If you positioned yourself at one of the venues, you could stay there for hours, watching each pageant wagon pull up in front of you, perform its play and then move on to make way for the next one.

The story so far

It is night, a short time before the birth of Jesus. The three shepherds have been watching their flocks, but have not been able to prevent a lamb being stolen by a local thief called Mak. The sheep-stealer runs back to his drunken wife, Gill, carrying the lamb under his arm.

Enter Mak at his house

MAK   Ho! Gill, art thou in?   Get us some light.

WIFE   Who makes such a din   this time of the night?

MAK   Good wife, open up quick!   Sees thou not what
       I bring?

WIFE   I will let thee draw the **sneck**.   Ah, come in
       my sweeting!

Mak shows her the sheep.

---

sneck latch.

MAK	Thus it fell to my lot, Gill; I had such grace.
WIFE	It were a foul blot to be hanged for that case.
MAK	I wish it were slain; I **list well** to eat:
	This twelvemonth was I not so fain
	for a slice **of sheep-meat.**
WIFE	Come they **ere** it be **slain**, and hear the sheep bleat . . .
MAK	Then might I be **tane**. That were a cold sweat! 10
	Go barr
	The back door.
WIFE	A good jest have I spied, since thou can find none:
	Here shall we him hide, until they be gone,
	In my cradle. **Abide!** Let me alone,
	And I shall sit down beside as in childbed, and groan.
	This is a good **guise**, **and a far-cast**;
	Still a woman's advice helps at the last.
MAK	The last word that they said when I turned my back:
	They would look that they had their sheep, all the
	pack. 20
	I think they will not be well pleased when they their
	sheep lack.
WIFE	Harken for when they call; they will come at once.
	Come, and make ready all, and sing on thine own;
	Sing 'Lullaby' thou shall, for I must groan,
	And cry out by the wall, on Mary and John.
	Full sore.

*The sheep bleats. Enter Shepherds and knock on
the door.*

I list well I would really like.
This twelvemonth . . . meat I haven't wanted a slice of sheep-meat so much all year.
ere before.
slain killed.
tane taken; arrested.
Abide! Stay there!
guise . . . cast trick.

MAK	Why, sir, **ails ye aught but good**?
1ST SHEP.	Yea, our sheep that we get
	Are stolen as they go. Our loss is great.
2ND SHEP.	Mak, some men suppose that it should be thee.
3RD SHEP.	Either thee or thy spouse, so say we.

                                                                                    30

MAK	Now if ye have suppose to Gill or to me,
	Come rip open our house, and then may ye see
	Who had her.
	If I any sheep got
	Either female or **stod** –
	And Gill, my wife, rose not
	Here since she laid her –
	As I am true and loyal, to God here I pray
	That this be the first meal that I shall eat
	this day.

He points to the cradle.   The sheep bleats.

WIFE	Ooh! My middle!
	I pray to God so mild,
	I ever I ye **beguild**
	That I *eat* this child
	That lies in this cradle.

                                                                                    40

MAK	Peace, woman, for God's pain, and cry not so!
	Thou spills all thy brain, and makes me full woe.
2ND SHEP.	I **trow** our sheep be slain. What find ye two?
3RD SHEP.	All work we in vain: as well may we go.
	Only tatters!
	I can find no flesh,

---

ails . . . good? is anything the matter?
stod ram.
beguild deceived.
trow believe.

Hard or **nesh**, 50
Salt or fresh –
    Only two empty platters.

(Pointing to cradle)

Living beast besides this,   tame or wild,
None, as have I bliss,   strong though it smelled.

WIFE   No. So God gi' me bliss.   And give me joy of my
    child!

1ST SHEP.   We have **marked amiss**.   I hold us beguild.

2ND SHEP.   Sir, we've done.
    But Sir – our Lady him save! –
    Is your child girl or **knave**?

MAK   Ay lord might him have, 60
    This child, to his son.

2ND SHEP.   Mak, friends will we be,   for we are all one.

MAK   We? Now I hold back, me,   for **amends** get I none.
    Fare well all three!   *(Aside)* All glad were ye gone.

The Shepherds leave the house.

3RD SHEP.   Fair words may there be,   but love is there none
    This year.

1ST SHEP.   Gave ye the child anything?

2ND SHEP.   I trow not one farthing.

3RD SHEP.   Fast again will I fling:
    Abide ye me there.

The Shepherds return.

---

nesh soft.
marked amiss made a mistake.
knave boy.
amends recompense; payment.

| | Mak, take it to no grief   if I come to thy **bairn**. | 70 |

MAK   Nay, thou does me great reproof,   and foul thyself
      borne.

3RD SHEP.   The child will not grieve,   that little **day-starne**.
      Mak, with your leave,   let me give your bairn
        But six pence.

MAK   Nay, have done.   He sleeps.

3RD SHEP.   Methinks he peeps.

MAK   When he wakens he weeps.
        I pray you go hence!

3RD SHEP.   Give me leave him to kiss, and lift up the **clout**.

      What the devil is this?   He has a long snout!

1ST SHEP.   He is marked amiss.   We should not pry about.   80

2ND SHEP.   Ill-spun **weft**, I **wis**,   ever comes foul out.
        Aye, so!
      He is like to our sheep.

3RD SHEP.   Ho, Gib, may I peep?

1ST SHEP.   I trow nature will creep
        Where it may not go.

2ND SHEP.   This was a quaint **gaud**,   and a far-cast;
      It was a fine fraud.

3RD SHEP.   Yea, sirs, was't.
      Let us burn this **bawd**   and bind her fast.
      A false scald   does hand at the last;
        So shall thou.   90

---

bairn child.
day-starne day-star.
clout cloth; blanket.
weft weave.
wis know.
gaud trick.
bawd harlot.

Will ye see how they swaddle
His four feet in the middle?
Saw I never in a cradle
     A horned lad ere now.

MAK   Peace, bid I. What,   let be your uproar!
I am he that him gat,   and yond woman
     him bare.

2ND SHEP.   Let be all that!   Now God send him care!
     I saw.

WIFE   As pretty child is he,
As e'er sits on woman's knee;
A **dillydon**, perdy,
     To cause a man laugh.   100

3RD SHEP.   I know him by the ear-mark: that is a sure token.

MAK   I tell you, sirs – hark! – his nose was broken.
And then told me a **clerk**   that witchcraft had
     spoken.

1ST SHEP.   This was a false work;   revenge must be **wreaken**.
     Get weapon!

WIFE   He was taken by an elf;
I saw it myself.
When the clock struck twelve
     Was he **forshapen**.

2ND SHEP.   Ye two are both **deft**,   and belong in one **stead**.

1ST SHEP.   Since they maintain their theft,   let us do them to
     death.   110

---

dillydon sweet little thing.
clerk scholar.
wreaken carried out.
forshapen misshapen; deformed.
deft clever.
stead place.

MAK   If I **trespass** here aft',   strike off my head.
         With you the matter be left.

3RD SHEP.   Sirs, do my rede:
        For this trespass
    We will neither ban nor flite,
    Fight nor chide
    But have done forthright.
    Set yon sheep thief in t'stocks . . .

---

trespass do wrong.

A7: Shakespeare in Love

Writers: Marc Norman and Tom Stoppard
Date: 1999
Staging: A film. The script is written in the form of a simplified screenplay (film script). The terms Int. and Ext. stand for 'interior' (a scene which takes place indoors) and 'exterior' (outdoors).
The story so far
This extract is the very beginning of the film. All we have had so far are the titles and the opening music.

Int. The Rose Theatre. Day.

SKY. Over which a title ' LONDON–SUMMER 1593' appears.

Title card: In the glory days of the Elizabethan theatre two playhouses were fighting it out for writers and audiences. North of the city was the Curtain Theatre, home to England's most famous actor, Richard Burbage. Across the river was the competition, built by Philip Henslowe, a businessman with a cash flow problem . . .

. . . The Rose . . .

Gradually a building is revealed, the Rose Theatre; three-tiered, open to the elements and empty. On the floor, roughly printed, a poster – torn, soiled, out of date. It says:

> SEPT. 7TH & 8TH AT NOON
> MR. EDWARD ALLEYN AND THE ADMIRAL'S MEN AT THE ROSE THEATRE,
> BANKSIDE
> THE LAMENTABLE TRAGEDIE OF THE MONEYLENDER REVENG'D

> *OVER THIS the screams of a man under torture.*

> *The screams are coming from the curtained stage.*

VOICE (O.S.) You Mongrel! Why do you howl
When it is I who am bitten?

Int. The Rose Theatre. Stage. Day.

> *The theatre owner, Philip Henslowe, is the man
screaming. Henslowe's boots are on fire. He is pinioned
in a chair, with his feet stuck out over the hot coals of a
fire burning in a brazier. He is being held in that position
by Lambert, who is a thug employed by Fennyman, who
is the owner of the voice. The fourth man, Frees, is
Fennyman's bookkeeper.*

FENNYMAN What am I, Mr Lambert?

LAMBERT Bitten, Mr Fennyman.

FENNYMAN How badly bitten, Mr Frees?

FREES Twelve pounds, one shilling and four pence,
Mr Fennyman, including interest.

HENSLOWE Aaagh! I can pay you!

FENNYMAN When?

HENSLOWE Two weeks, three at the most, Aaagh!
For pity's sake!

FENNYMAN Take his feet out. Where will you get . . .

FREES *(the mathematical genius with a notebook)* Sixteen
pounds, five shillings and nine pence . . .

FENNYMAN . . . including interest in three weeks?

HENSLOWE I have a wonderful new play!

FENNYMAN Put his feet in.

HENSLOWE It's a comedy.

FENNYMAN	Cut his nose off.
HENSLOWE	A new comedy. By Will Shakespeare!
FENNYMAN	And his ears.
HENSLOWE	And a share. We will be partners, Mr Fennyman!
FENNYMAN	*(hesitating)* Partners?
HENSLOWE	It's a crowd-tickler – mistaken identities, a shipwreck, a pirate king, a bit with a dog, and love triumphant.
LAMBERT	I think I've seen it. I didn't like it.
HENSLOWE	This time it is by Shakespeare.
FENNYMAN	What's the title?
HENSLOWE	*Romeo and Ethel the Pirate's Daughter.*
FENNYMAN	Good title.

Fennyman snaps his fingers at Frees and Lambert. Lambert unties Henslowe, Frees starts writing a contract.

	A play takes time. Find actors . . . rehearsals . . . let's say open in three weeks. That's – what – five hundred groundlings at tuppence each, in addition four hundred backsides at three pence – a penny extra for a cushion, call it two hundred cushions, say two performance for safety – how much is that Mr Frees?
FREES	Twenty pounds to the penny, Mr Fennyman.
FENNYMAN	Correct!
HENSLOWE	But I have to pay the actors and the author.
FENNYMAN	A share of the profits.
HENSLOWE	There's never any . . .
FENNYMAN	Of course not!
HENSLOWE	*(impressed)* Mr. Fennyman, I think you may have hit on something.

Fennyman slaps a contract down on the table next to an ink-pot and quill.

FENNYMAN   Sign here.

Henslowe takes the quill and signs.

Romeo and Ethel the Pirate's Daughter . . . Almost finished?

HENSLOWE   Without doubt he is completing it at this very moment.

Int. Will's Room. Day.

A small cramped space in the eaves of a building. A cluttered shelf containing various objects, wedged between crumpled pieces of paper. Among those we have time to observe: a skull, a mug that says ' A PRESENT FROM STRATFORD-UPON-AVON' .

At infreqent intervals, further pieces of crumpled paper are tossed towards the shelf. The man who is throwing them, Will Shakespeare, is bent over a table, writing studiously with a quill.

Now we see what he is writing: Will is practising his signature, over and over again. ' Will Shagsbeard . . . W. Shakspur . . . William Shasper . . .' Each time he is dissatisfied, and each time he crumples, and tosses it away.

Suddenly Will becomes impatient. He jumps up and goes to the loft area in the rafters, where he sleeps, and starts to pull on his boots. At this point the door opens and Henslowe walks in. He is out of breath and his feet hurt.

HENSLOWE   Will! Where is my play? Tell me you have it nearly
           done!
           Tell me you have it started.
           (Desperately) You have begun?

WILL   *(struggling with his boots)* Doubt that the stars are
           fire, doubt that the sun doth move . . .

HENSLOWE   No, no, we haven't the time. Talk prose. Where is
           my play?

WILL   *(tapping his forehead and heading out the door)*
           It is all locked safe in here.

HENSLOWE   God be praised!
           (Then doubt) Locked?

WILL   As soon as I have found my muse . . .

A8: Educating Rita

Writer: Willy Russell
Date: 1980
Staging: Realistic sets, props and costumes. This scene needs to look like the study of a university lecturer – untidy and full of books.
(*Educating Rita* was also a very successful film, starring Julie Walters and Michael Caine.)

The story so far

Rita, a hairdresser who did not receive much education at school, has enrolled with the Open University to study for a degree. University is a completely different world for her and she is having to cope with its strangeness as well as opposition from her husband, who thinks that her ambition to study is ridiculous. This meeting between Rita and her tutor Frank takes place only a short way into the play.

Scene Six

> *Frank enters, carrying a briefcase and a pile of essays. He goes to the filing cabinet, takes his lecture notes from the briefcase and puts them in a drawer. He takes the sandwiches and apple from his briefcase and puts them on his desk and then goes to the window desk and dumps the essays and briefcase. He switches on the radio and then sits in the swivel chair. He opens the packet of sandwiches, takes a bite and then picks up a book and starts reading.*
>
> *Rita bursts through the door out of breath.*

FRANK   What are you doing here? *(He looks at his watch.)* It's Thursday, you . . .

RITA   *(moving over to the desk, quickly)* I know I shouldn't be here, it's me dinner hour, but listen, I've gorra tell someone, have y' got a few minutes, can y' spare . . .?

FRANK   *(alarmed)* My God, what is it?

RITA   I had to come an' tell y', Frank, last night, I went to the theatre! A proper one, a professional theatre.

Frank gets up and switches off the radio and then returns to the swivel chair.

FRANK   *(sighing)* For God's sake, you had me worried, I thought it was something serious.   10

RITA   No, listen, it was. I went out an' got me ticket, it was Shakespeare, I thought it was gonna be dead borin' . . .

FRANK   Then why did you go in the first place?

RITA   I wanted to find out. But listen, it wasn't borin', it was bleedin' great, honest, ogh, it done me in, it was fantastic. I'm gonna do an essay on it.

FRANK   *(smiling)* Come on, which one was it?

Rita moves upper right centre.

RITA   '. . . Out, out, brief candle!
Life's but a walking shadow, a poor player   20
That struts and frets his hour upon the stage
And then is heard no more. It is a tale
Told by an idiot, full of sound and fury
Signifying nothing.'

FRANK   *(deliberately)* Ah, *Romeo and Juliet*.

RITA   *(moving towards Frank)* Tch. Frank! Be serious. I learnt that today from the book. *(She produces a copy of Macbeth.)* Look, I went out an' bought the book. Isn't it great! What I couldn't get over is how excitin' it was.

Frank puts his feet up on the desk.

RITA   Wasn't his wife a cow, eh? An' that fantastic bit where he meets Macduff an' he thinks he's all invincible. I was on   30 the edge of me seat at that bit. I wanted to shout out an' tell Macbeth, warn him.

FRANK   You didn't, did you?

RITA   Nah. Y' can't do that in a theatre, can y'? It was dead good. It was like a thriller.

FRANK   Yes. You'll have to go and see more.

RITA   I'm goin' to. Macbeth's a tragedy, isn't it?

Frank nods.

RITA   Right.

Rita smiles at Frank and he smiles back at her.

Well I just – I just had to tell someone who'd understand.

FRANK   I'm honoured that you chose me.   40

RITA   *(moving towards the door)* Well, I better get back. I've left a customer with a perm lotion. If I don't get a move on there'll be another tragedy.

FRANK   No. There won't be a tragedy.

RITA   There will, y'know. I know this woman; she's dead fussy. If her perm doesn't come out right there'll be blood an' guts everywhere.

FRANK   Which might be quite tragic – *(He throws her the apple from his desk which she catches.)* – but it won't be a tragedy.

RITA   What!   50

FRANK   Well – erm – look; the tragedy of the drama has nothing to do with the sort of tragic event you're talking about. Macbeth is flawed by his ambition – yes?

RITA   *(going and sitting in the chair by the desk)* Yeh. Go on. *(She starts to eat the apple.)*

FRANK   Erm – it's that flaw which forces him to take the inevitable steps towards his own doom. You see?

Rita offers him the can of soft drink. He takes it and looks at it.

FRANK *(putting the can down on the desk)* No thanks. Whereas, Rita, a woman's hair being reduced to an inch of stubble, or – or the sort of thing you read in the paper that's reported as being tragic, 'Man Killed By Falling Tree', is not a tragedy.   60

RITA It is for the poor sod under the tree.

FRANK Yes, it's tragic, absolutely tragic. But it's not a tragedy in the way that *Macbeth* is a tragedy. Tragedy in dramatic terms is inevitable, pre-ordained. Look, now, even without ever having heard the story of *Macbeth* you wanted to shout out, to warn him and prevent him going on, didn't you? But you wouldn't have been able to stop him, would you?

RITA No.   70

FRANK Why?

RITA They would have thrown me out the theatre.

FRANK But what I mean is that your warning would have been ignored. He's warned in the play. But he can't go back. He still treads the path to doom. But the poor old fellow under the tree hasn't arrived there by following any inevitable steps, has he?

RITA No.

FRANK There's no particular flaw in his character that has dictated his end. If he'd been warned of the   80 consequences of standing beneath that particular tree he wouldn't have done it, would he? Understand?

RITA So – so Macbeth brings it on himself?

FRANK Yes. You see, he goes blindly on and on and with every step he's spinning one more piece of thread which will eventually make up the network of his own tragedy. Do you see?

RITA	I think so. I'm not used to thinkin' like this.
FRANK	It's quite easy, Rita.
RITA	It is for you. I just thought it was a dead excitin' story. 90 But the way you tell it you make me see all sorts of things in it. *(After a pause)* It's fun, tragedy, isn't it? *(She goes over to the window.)* All them out there, they know all about that sort of thing, don't they?
FRANK	Look, how about a proper lunch?
RITA	Lunch? *(She leaps up, grabs the copy of* Macbeth, *the can of drink and the apple and goes to the door.)* Christ – me customer. She only wanted a demi-wave – she'll come out looking like a friggin' muppet. *(She comes back to the table.)* Ey' Frank, listen – I was thinkin' of goin' to the 100 art gallery tomorrow. It's me half-day off. D' y' wanna come with me?
FRANK	*(smiling)* All right.

Rita goes to the door.

FRANK	*(looking at her)* And – look, what are you doing on Saturday?
RITA	I work.
FRANK	Well, when you finish work?
RITA	Dunno.
FRANK	I want you to come over to the house.
RITA	Why? 110
FRANK	Julia's organised a few people to come round for dinner.
RITA	An' y' want me to come? Why?
FRANK	Why do you think?
RITA	I dunno.
FRANK	Because you might enjoy it.

RITA   Oh.

FRANK   Will you come?

RITA   If y' want.

FRANK   What do you want?

RITA   All right. I'll come.

FRANK   Will you bring Denny?

RITA   I don't know if he'll come.

FRANK   Well, ask him.

RITA   *(puzzled)* All right.

FRANK   What's wrong?

RITA   What shall I wear?

Blackout. Rita goes out.

A9: The Importance of Being Earnest

Writer: Oscar Wilde
Date: 1895
Staging: A theatre with a proscenium (picture-frame) stage. A realistic set, costumes and props.

The story so far

John Worthing (Jack) is in love with Gwendolen Fairfax. In this scene, he has asked Gwendolen's terrifying aunt, Lady Bracknell, for permission to marry Gwendolen. Lady Bracknell proceeds to ask him some important questions.

LADY BRACKNELL	*(sitting down)* You can take a seat, Mr Worthing.
	Looks in her pocket for note-book and pencil.
JACK	Thank you, Lady Bracknell, I prefer standing.
LADY BRACKNELL	*(pencil and note-book in hand)* I feel bound to tell you that you are not down on my list of eligible young men, although I have the same list as the dear Duchess of Bolton has. We work together, in fact. However, I am quite ready to enter your name, should your answers be what a really affectionate mother requires. Do you smoke?
JACK	Well, yes, I must admit I smoke.
LADY BRACKNELL	I am glad to hear it. A man should always have an occupation of some kind. There are far too many idle men in London as it is. How old are you?
JACK	Twenty-nine.
LADY BRACKNELL	A very good age to be married at. I have always been of opinion that a man who desires to get married should know either everything or nothing. Which do you know?

JACK	*(after some hesitation)* I know nothing, Lady Bracknell.
LADY BRACKNELL	I am pleased to hear it. I do not approve of anything that tampers with natural ignorance. Ignorance is like a delicate exotic fruit; touch it and the bloom is gone. The whole theory of modern education is radically unsound. Fortunately in England, at any rate, education produces no effect whatsoever. If it did, it would prove a serious danger to the upper classes, and probably lead to acts of violence in Grosvenor Square. What is your income?
JACK	Between seven and eight thousand a year.
LADY BRACKNELL	*(makes a note in her book)* In land, or in investments?
JACK	In investments, chiefly.
LADY BRACKNELL	That is satisfactory. What between the duties expected of one during one's lifetime, and the duties exacted from one after one's death, land has ceased to be either a profit or a pleasure. It gives one position, and prevents one from keeping it up. That's all that can be said about land.
JACK	I have a country house with some land, of course, attached to it, about fifteen hundred acres, I believe; but I don't depend on that for my real income. In fact, as far as I can make out, the poachers are the only people who make anything out of it.
LADY BRACKNELL	A country house! How many bedrooms? Well, that point can be cleared up afterwards. You have a town house, I hope? A girl with a simple,

unspoiled nature, like Gwendolen, could hardly be expected to reside in the country.

JACK   Well, I own a house in Belgrave Square, but it is let by the year to Lady Bloxham. Of course, I can get it back whenever I like, at six months' notice.

LADY BRACKNELL   Lady Bloxham? I don't know her.

JACK   Oh, she goes about very little. She is a lady considerably advanced in years.

LADY BRACKNELL   Ah, nowadays that is no guarantee of respectability of character. What number in Belgrave Square.

JACK   149

LADY BRACKNELL   *(shaking her head)* The unfashionable side. I thought there was something. However, that could easily be altered.

JACK   Do you mean the fashion, or the side?

LADY BRACKNELL   *(sternly)* Both, if necessary, I presume. What are your politics?

JACK   Well, I am afraid I really have none. I am a Liberal Unionist.

LADY BRACKNELL   Oh, they count as Tories. They dine with us. Or come in the evening, at any rate. Now to minor matters. Are your parents living?

JACK   I have lost both my parents.

LADY BRACKNELL   To lose one parent, Mr Worthing, may be regarded as a misfortune; to lose both looks like carelessness. Who was your father? He was evidently a man of some wealth. Was he born in what the Radical papers call the purple of commerce, or did he rise from the ranks of the aristocracy?

JACK	I am afraid I really don't know. The fact is, Lady Bracknell, I said I had lost my parents. It would be nearer the truth to say that my parents seem to have lost me . . . I don't actually know who I am by birth. I was . . . well, I was found.
LADY BRACKNELL	Found!
JACK	The late Mr Thomas Cardew, an old gentleman of a very charitable and kindly disposition, found me, and gave me the name of Worthing, because he happened to have a first-class ticket for Worthing in his pocket at the time. Worthing is a place in Sussex. It is a seaside resort.
LADY BRACKNELL	Where did the charitable gentleman who had a first-class ticket for this seaside resort find you?
JACK	*(gravely)* In a hand-bag.
LADY BRACKNELL	A hand-bag?
JACK	*(very seriously)* Yes, Lady Bracknell. I was in a hand-bag – a somewhat large, black leather hand-bag, with handles to it – an ordinary hand-bag in fact.
LADY BRACKNELL	In what locality did this Mr James, or Thomas, Cardew come across this ordinary hand-bag.
JACK	In the cloak-room at Victoria Station. It was given to him in mistake for his own.
LADY BRACKNELL	The cloak-room at Victoria Station?
JACK	Yes. The Brighton line.
LADY BRACKNELL	The line is immaterial. Mr. Worthing, I confess I feel somewhat bewildered by what you have just told me. To be born, or at any rate bred, in a hand-bag, whether it had handles or not, seems to me to display a contempt for the ordinary decencies of family life that reminds

one of the worst excesses of the French Revolution. And I presume you know what that unfortunate movement led to? As for the particular locality in which the hand-bag was found, a cloak-room at a railway station might serve to conceal a social indiscretion – has probably, indeed, been used for that purpose before now – but it could hardly be regarded as an assured basis for a recognised position in good society.

JACK May I ask you then what you would advise me to do? I need hardly say I would do anything in the world to ensure Gwendolen's happiness.

LADY BRACKNELL I would strongly advise you, Mr Worthing, to try and acquire some relations as soon as possible, and to make a definite effort to produce at any rate one parent, of either sex, before the season is quite over.

JACK Well, I don't see how I could possibly manage to do that. I can produce the hand-bag at any moment. It is in my dressing-room at home. I really think that should satisfy you, Lady Bracknell.

LADY BRACKNELL Me, sir! What has it to do with me? You can hardly imagine that I and Lord Bracknell would dream of allowing our only daughter – a girl brought up with the utmost care – to marry into a cloak-room, and form an alliance with a parcel. Good morning, Mr Worthing!

A10: Fawlty Towers

Writers: Connie Booth and John Cleese
Date: 1975
Staging: Television.

The story so far

Hotel owner Basil Fawlty has gone away for the night with his wife, Sybil, leaving the hotel to be run by his young assistant Polly and the Spanish waiter, Manuel. Before he left, Basil arranged for some builders to come in to do some work in the lobby, blocking off one doorway and opening up a new one. Sybil thinks that Basil has made arrangements with the efficient builder, Stubbs. In fact, he has asked the bungling O'Reilly to do the job because he is a lot cheaper. When this scene opens, Polly is drawing a picture of Manuel.

In the lobby, later that day. Manuel is posing for Polly.

MANUEL	Oh, Polly, finish, I *tired*.
POLLY	Oh, that's wonderful, Manuel – just hold it a second.
MANUEL	*Que?*
POLLY	*Quiero ascender para dormir.*
MANUEL	No, no – you must speak me English. Is good. I learn.
POLLY	I want to go upstairs in a moment.
MANUEL	*Que?*
POLLY	*(pointing)* I . . . go upstairs . . .
MANUEL	*Si*. Is easy
POLLY	For a little sleep.
MANUEL	Is difficult.
POLLY	For siesta.
MANUEL	Siesta . . . little sleep?
POLLY	Yes.

MANUEL	Same in Spanish.
POLLY	When O'Reilly's men come, you must wake me.
MANUEL	When Orrible men . . . ? *(Looks alarmed.)*
POLLY	Now Manuel, listen. When men come here . . . Señor O'Reilly . . .
MANUEL	When men come . . .
POLLY	You come upstairs and wake me up . . . *despierteme.*
MANUEL	Ah! When men come, I . . . vendre arriba para despertartle en su cuarto.
POLLY	Antes que ellos comienzan a trabajar aqui, si?
MANUEL	Comprendo, comprendo.
POLLY	Finished!

She finishes the sketch and disappears upstairs. Manuel relaxes from his pose. He goes behind the reception desk and enjoys his new responsibility. He rings the desk bell in an imperious manner.

MANUEL	Manuel! *(Picks up the phone, although it has not rung.)* Manuel Towers. How are you. Is nice today. Goodbye. *(Rings off as he sees Bennion the delivery man arriving, complete with a rather large garden gnome.)* Ah! Hallo. Good day! How are you?
BENNION	*(referring to delivery note)* Number sixteen?
MANUEL	*(consulting the register)* Si, si, sixtcen. But no eat.
BENNION	What?
MANUEL	Sixteen is free. But not possible . . . *(Mimes eating.)*
BENNION	*(indicating the hotel generally)* Is this . . . number sixteen?
MANUEL	No, no, this . . . lobby. Sixteen upstairs, on right.
BENNION	Who's in charge here?
MANUEL	No, no, charge later. After sleep.
BENNION	Where's the boss?

MANUEL	Boss is, er . . . Oh! *I* boss!
BENNION	No, no, where's the *real* boss?
MANUEL	*Que?*
BENNION	The . . . the generalissimo.
MANUEL	In Madrid.
BENNION	Look, just sign this, will you?
MANUEL	*(signing the note)* Si, si . . . er . . . sixteen?
BENNION	What?
MANUEL	You want room sixteen.
BENNION	No, I *don't* want a room, mate, I'm just leaving *him*, right? *(Points at the gnome and walks out.)*
MANUEL	You want room sixteen . . . for *him*?
BENNION	*(as he leaves)* Yeah, with a bath, you dago twit.
MANUEL	*(calling after him)* You mad! You . . . *mad* . . . You pay for room first . . . He crazy! *(He picks up the gnome.)* Room 16 . . . No pay, no room sixteen.

He puts the gnome out of sight behind the desk. The phone rings; as he goes to answer it, O' Reilly's men – Lurphy, Jones, and Kerr – enter.

MANUEL	*(to phone)* Hallo, Fawlty Towers. How are you, is nice day . . . No, he not here . . . No, no, he *not* here, very very sorry, goodbye. *(Rings off; to the men)* Hallo, men.
LURPHY	Good day, now. *(He is Irish.)*
MANUEL	You are men?
LURPHY	*(dangerously)* You what!
MANUEL	. . . You are men?
LURPHY	*(threateningly)* Are you trying to be funny?
MANUEL	What . . . ?
LURPHY	I said, 'Are you trying to be funny?'

KERR	*(restraining him)* Not here, Spud, not here.
MANUEL	But, you are men with Orelly?
JONES	. . . What?
MANUEL	You are Orelly men?
LURPHY	*(menacingly)* What does *that* mean?
MANUEL	You Orelly.
LURPHY	You watch it!
MANUEL	. . . Where Orelly?
JONES	What's he going on about?
KERR	He means O'Reilly.
LURPHY	*(understanding at last)* Oh yes, that's right, yes – we are Orelly men. *(To his companions)* Thick as a plank.
MANUEL	You wait here, please, I go . . . *(Indicates upstairs; the phone rings; he answers it.)* You wait too, please.

He puts the phone down, hurries upstairs and knocks on the door of Polly's room. There is no response; he knocks again. He opens the door quietly and looks inside. Polly is on the bed, fast asleep.

(whispering) Polly . . . Polly . . .

But she is in a very deep sleep so he decides to take care of things himself. Back in the lobby, the men are looking around. The phone is ringing; Manuel rushes down the stairs and answers it.

Hello, Fawlty Towers, how are you, is nice day . . . oh, you again! No, I say he is not here, very very sorry, goodbye. *(Rings off.)* Choh! Choh!

The men are consulting the plan.

You men know what to do?

JONES	Oh, I think so. This is the dining room?

MANUEL	*(nods)* . . . You are certain you know?
JONES	It looks pretty straightforward. We've just got to block this one off.

The phone rings again. Manuel answers it.

MANUEL	Yes, yes, yes . . . Is you again! Listen! He not here! How many times? Where are your ears? You great big . . . hhhalf wit, I tell you, he *not here!* Listen! *(He holds the receiver out so that the caller may register the lack of Basilic noises.)* Now you understand? . . . *(Sudden comprehension and horror.)* Oh, Mr Fawlty! I very sorry!! I very sorry . . . is you . . . yes, is me, Mr Fawlty . . . No, no, Polly is . . . she very busy . . . Men? Yes, yes, the men are here . . . *(To men, imperiously)* You work, men . . . *(To phone)* Yes . . . Man with beard? *(To men)* Please, which one is man with beard?

Lurphy, who is the only bearded one, thinks this over for a bit and then indicates himself.

(To phone) . . . Yes . . . hid . . . o . . . angtang . . . tag . . . tang . . . si . . . one moment, please. *(Puts the receiver on the desk and addresses Lurphy.)* You are a hid . . . eous . . . orang . . . tang. *(He bows; Lurphy hits him.)*

BASIL'S VOICE	*(from the phone)* Well done, Manuel. Thank you very much. *(Dialling tone is heard.)*

The next morning; it is a lovely day. Outside the hotel, birds are singing, moles frolic, weasels dance the hornpipe. Polly is still fast asleep in her room. Outside, Basil's car draws up. He leaps out and runs up the steps. He strides into the lobby.

BASIL	Polly?

He goes to the wall by the stairs where the new door to the kitchen should be . . . it isn't. He looks around to the door to the drawing room to see if it is blocked off. It isn't.

BASIL	Polly! Polly!!

He opens the new door at the foot of the stairs and is halfway up the flight when he registers that this is wrong. He comes back and examines the door with mounting fury.

BASIL	. . . Polly!! Polly!!! . . . *Manuel!!!*

He makes for the dining-room door . . . but there is now a blank wall there. Polly has just opened the stairs door and sees his apoplectic reaction. She tries to close the door quietly but he has seen her.

BASIL	What have you done with my hotel?! Polly!! . . . What have you done to my hotel?
POLLY	What?

He grabs her by the ear and shows her the stairs door.

BASIL	Look!
POLLY	Oh, it's nice. I like it there. *(He leads her, lobe first, to the late dining-room door.)* Ow! You're hurting me. *(She escapes the ear-lock.)*
BASIL	What have you done with my dining-room door? Where is it?
POLLY	I don't know.
BASIL	*Why* don't you know? I left you in charge.
POLLY	Oh . . . I fell asleep.
BASIL	You fell *asleep!!*
POLLY	It's not my fault.
BASIL	You fell *asleep*, and it's *not your fault!!*?
POLLY	He forgot to wake me.
BASIL	Who forgot to wake you?
POLLY	. . . It *is* my fault.
BASIL	Manuel!!! I knew it!

POLLY	Don't blame him.
BASIL	Why not?
POLLY	It wasn't really his fault.
BASIL	Well, whose fault is it then, you cloth-eared bint – *Denis Compton's?!!!*
POLLY	Well, you hired O'Reilly, didn't you?

A pause; Basil's eyes go oddly glazed.

POLLY	We all warned you . . . who else would do something like this?
BASIL	. . . I beg your pardon?
POLLY	You hired O'Reilly . . .
BASIL	. . . Oh! Oh, I *see!* . . . It's *my* fault, is it? . . . Oh, of course, there I was, thinking it was your fault because you had been left in charge, or *Manuel's* fault for not waking you, and all the time it was *my* fault! Oh, it's so obvious now, I've seen the light. Ah well, if it's my fault, I must be punished then, mustn't I? *(Slaps his bottom.)* You're a naughty boy, Fawlty! Don't do it again! *(He catches himself a real cracker across the head, staggers, and straightens up.)* . . . What am I going to do? She'll be back at lunch time!
POLLY	Now wait . . .
BASIL	I'm a dead man, do you realise?
POLLY	*(soothingly)* Easy! . . .
BASIL	You're dead too. We're *all dead!!* *(He is quivering violently.)*
POLLY	Don't panic.
BASIL	What *else* is there to do? *(Starts crying.)*
POLLY	We'll call O'Reilly – he made this mess, he can clear it up! *(Basil has not taken this in; she shakes him.)* Oh, just pull yourself together. *(Shakes him again.)* Come on! Come on!

But he is worse. She pauses, takes a step back, then slaps his face. He goes to hit her back, then realises it has done him some good.

BASIL   . . . Again! *(She slaps him, rather deferentially.)* . . . Harder!! *(She slaps him really hard.)* Right! I'll call O'Reilly.

A11: Pygmalion

Writer: George Bernard Shaw
Date: 1913
Staging: Realistic sets, props and costumes.

The story so far

Professor Henry Higgins, an expert on accents and dialects, has made a bet that he can teach the common flower-girl Eliza Doolittle to speak so 'correctly' that people in high society will believe she is a duchess. In this scene, after teaching Eliza for some time, Higgins takes her to his mother's house, where she is entertaining a number of her high-society friends. He enters first, so that the beautifully dressed Eliza can arrive with the maximum of impact. But will she speak correctly enough to fool them . . .?

PARLOUR-MAID   *(opening the door)* Miss Doolittle. *(She withdraws.)*

HIGGINS   *(rising hastily and turning to Mrs Higgins)* Here she is, mother. *(He stands on tiptoe and makes signs over his mother's head to Eliza to indicate to her which lady is her hostess.)*

Eliza, who is exquisitely dressed, produces an impression of such remarkable distinction and beauty as she enters that they all rise, quite fluttered. Guided by Higgins's signals, she comes to Mrs Higgins with studied grace.

LIZA   *(speaking with pedantic correctness of pronunciation and great beauty of tone)* How do you do, Mrs Higgins? *(She gasps slightly in making sure of the H in Higgins, but is quite successful.)* Mr Higgins told me I might come.

MRS HIGGINS	*(cordially)* Quite right: I'm very glad indeed to see you.
PICKERING	How do you do, Miss Doolittle?
LIZA	*(shaking hands with him)* Colonel Pickering, is it not?
MRS EYNSFORD HILL	I feel sure we have met before, Miss Doolittle. I remember your eyes.
LIZA	How do you do? *(She sits down on the ottoman gracefully in the place just left vacant by Higgins.)*
MRS EYNSFORD HILL	*(introducing)* My daughter Clara.
LIZA	How do you do?
CLARA	*(impulsively)* How do you do? *(She sits down on the ottoman beside Eliza, devouring her with her eyes.)*
FREDDY	*(coming to their side of the ottoman)* I've certainly had the pleasure.
MRS EYNSFORD HILL	*(introducing)* My son Freddy.
LIZA	How do you do?
	Freddy bows and sits down in the Elizabethan chair, infatuated.
HIGGINS	*(suddenly)* By George, yes: it all comes back to me! *(They stare at him.)* Covent Garden! *(Lamentably)* What a damned thing!
MRS HIGGINS	Henry, please! *(He is about to sit on the edge of the table.)* Don't sit on my writing-table: you'll break it.
HIGGINS	*(sulkily)* Sorry.
	He goes to the divan, stumbling into the fender and over the fire-irons on his way; extricating himself with muttered imprecations; and finishing his disastrous journey by throwing

10

20

himself so impatiently on the divan that he
almost breaks it. Mrs Higgins looks at him, but
controls herself and says nothing. A long and
painful pause ensues.

MRS HIGGINS *(at last, conversationally)* Will it rain, do you think? 30

LIZA The shallow depression in the west of these islands is likely to move slowly in an easterly direction. There are no indications of any great change in the barometrical situation.

FREDDY Ha! ha! how awfully funny!

LIZA What is wrong with that, young man? I bet I got it right.

FREDDY Killing!

MRS EYNSFORD HILL I'm sure I hope it won't turn cold. There's so much influenza about. It runs right 40
through our whole family regularly every spring.

LIZA *(darkly)* My aunt died of influenza: so they said.

MRS EYNSFORD HILL *(clicks her tongue sympathetically)* !!!

LIZA *(in the same tragic tone)* But it's my belief they done the old woman in.

MRS HIGGINS *(puzzled)* Done her in?

LIZA Y-e-e-e-es, Lord love you! Why should she die of influenza? She come through diphtheria right enough the year before. I saw her with 50
my own eyes. Fairly blue with it, she was. They all thought she was dead; but my father he kept ladling gin down her throat till she came to so sudden that she bit the bowl off the spoon.

MRS EYNSFORD HILL *(startled)* Dear me!

LIZA	*(piling up the indictment)* What call would a woman with that strength in her have to die of influenza? What become of her new straw hat that should have come to me? Somebody 60 pinched it; and what I say is, them as pinched it done her in.
MRS EYNSFORD HILL	What does 'doing her in' mean?
HIGGINS	*(hastily)* Oh, that's the new small talk. To do a person in means to kill them.
MRS EYNSFORD HILL	*(to Eliza, horrified)* You surely don't believe that your aunt was killed?
LIZA	Do I not! Them she lived with would have killed her for a hat-pin, let alone a hat.
MRS EYNSFORD HILL	But it can't have been right for your father to 70 pour spirits down her throat like that. It might have killed her.
LIZA	Not her. Gin was mother's milk to her. Besides, he'd poured so much down his own throat that he knew the good of it.
MRS EYNSFORD HILL	Do you mean that he drank?
LIZA	Drank! My word! Something chronic.
MRS EYNSFORD HILL	How dreadful for you!
LIZA	Not a bit. It never did him no harm what I could see. But then he did not keep it up 80 regular. *(Cheerfully)* On the burst, as you might say, from time to time. And always more agreeable when he had a drop in. When he was out of work, my mother used to give him fourpence and tell him to go out and not come back until he'd drunk himself cheerful and loving-like. There's lots of women has to make their husbands drunk to make them fit to live with. *(Now quite at her*

ease.) You see, it's like this. If a man has a bit 90
of a conscience, it always takes him when
he's sober; and then it makes him low-
spirited. A drop of booze just takes that off
and makes him happy. *(To Freddy, who is in
convulsions of suppressed laughter)* Here! What
are you sniggering at?

FREDDY The new small talk! You do it so awfully well.

LIZA If I was doing it proper, what was you laughing
at? *(To Higgins)* Have I said anything, I oughtn't?

MRS HIGGINS *(interposing)* Not at all, Miss Doolittle. 100

LIZA Well, that's a mercy, anyhow. *(Expansively)*
What I always say is –

HIGGINS *(rising and looking at his watch)* Ahem!

LIZA *(looking round at him; taking the hint; and rising)*
Well: I must go. *(They all rise. Freddy goes to the
door.)* So pleased to have met you. Goodbye.
(She shakes hands with Mrs Higgins.)

MRS HIGGINS Goodbye.

LIZA Goodbye, Colonel Pickering.

PICKERING Goodbye, Miss Doolittle.

They shake hands.

LIZA *(nodding to the others)* Goodbye, all

FREDDY *(opening the door for her)* Are you walking 110
across the Park, Miss Doolittle? If so –

LIZA *(with perfectly elegant diction)* Walk! Not bloody
likely. *(Sensation)* I am going in a taxi. *(She
goes out.)*

*Pickering gasps and sits down. Freddy goes
out on the balcony to catch another glimpse
of Eliza.*

A12: The Rivals

Writer: Richard Brinsley Sheridan
Date: 1775
Staging: A theatre with a proscenium (picture-frame) stage. A painted backdrop, but realistic costumes and props.

The story so far

Captain Jack Absolute is in love with Lydia Languish, the niece of Mrs Malaprop. The problem is, the romantic Lydia is determined to marry someone poor, so Jack has pretended to be a low-ranking soldier, Ensign Beverley. The other problem is that Lydia cannot marry without Mrs Malaprop's consent, so Jack has to approach Mrs Malaprop as his real (wealthy) self, claiming that he has never met Lydia, and explaining that the marriage has been arranged by his father. In this scene, Jack meets Mrs Malaprop for the first time, only to find that she has intercepted one of the letters he has written to Lydia under the name of 'Ensign Beverley'!

ACT III

Scene 3 Mrs Malaprop's lodgings

Mrs Malaprop and Captain Absolute

MRS MALAPROP   Your being Sir Anthony's son, Captain, would itself be a sufficient accommodation; but from the **ingenuity** of your appearance, I am convinced you deserve the character here given of you.

ABSOLUTE   Permit me to say, Madam, that as I never yet have had the pleasure of seeing Miss Languish, my **principal inducement** in this affair at present, is the honour of being allied to Mrs Malaprop; of

---

ingenuity cleverness; but she means 'ingenuousness' (openness; innocence).
my principal inducement the main point that attracts me.

whose intellectual accomplishments, elegant manners, and unaffected learning, no tongue is silent.

MRS MALAPROP Sir, you do me infinite honour! I beg, Captain, you'll be seated. *(They sit.)* Ah! few gentlemen, nowadays, know how to value the **ineffectual** qualities in a woman! Few think how a little knowledge becomes a gentlewoman! Men have no sense now but for the worthless flower of beauty!

ABSOLUTE It is but too true indeed, Ma'am – yet I fear our ladies should share the blame – they think our admiration of beauty so great, that knowledge in them would be **superfluous**. Thus, like garden-trees, they seldom show fruit, till time has robbed them of the more **specious** blossom. Few, like Mrs Malaprop and the orange-tree, are rich in both at once!

MRS MALAPROP Sir – you overpower me with good-breeding. He is the very **pineapple** of politeness! You are not ignorant, Captain, that this giddy girl has somehow contrived to fix her affections on a beggarly, strolling, eavesdropping Ensign, whom none of us have seen, and nobody knows anything of.

ABSOLUTE Oh, I have heard the silly affair before. I'm not at all prejudiced against her on that account.

MRS MALAPROP You are very good, and very considerate, Captain. I am sure I have done everything in my power since I exploded the affair! Long ago I laid my positive

---

ineffectual fruitless; she means 'intellectual'.
superfluous more than is necessary.
specious seeming good but lacking real value.
pineapple she means 'pinnacle' (the highest point).

	conjunctions on her never to think on the fellow again – I have since laid Sir Anthony's preposition before her – but I'm sorry to say she seems resolved to decline every particle that I enjoin her.
ABSOLUTE	It must be very distressing indeed, Ma'am.
MRS MALAPROP	Oh! it gives me the hydrostatics to such a degree! I thought she had persisted from corresponding with him; but behold this very day, I have interceded another letter from the fellow! I believe I have it in my pocket.
ABSOLUTE	*(aside)* Oh the devil! my last note.
MRS MALAPROP	Aye, here it is.
ABSOLUTE	*(aside)* Aye, my note indeed! O the little traitress Lucy.
MRS MALAPROP	There, perhaps, you may know the writing. *(Gives him the letter.)*
ABSOLUTE	I think I have seen the hand before – yes, I certainly must have seen this hand before –
MRS MALAPROP	Nay, but read it, Captain.
ABSOLUTE	*(reads)* 'My soul's idol, my adored Lydia!' Very tender indeed!
MRS MALAPROP	Tender! aye, and profane too, o' my conscience!
ABSOLUTE	'I am excessively alarmed at the intelligence you send me, the more so as my new rival –'

---

conjunctions . . .preposition . . . particle three grammatical terms; she means
'injunctions' (orders); 'proposition' (suggestion; plan) and 'article' (point, item).
hydrostatics science to do with liquids; she means 'hysterics' (fits of extreme
emotion).
persisted carried on; she means 'desisted' (stopped).
interceded acted as a go-between; she means 'intercepted' (caught going from one
place to another).
profane irreverent.
intelligence information.

MRS MALAPROP	That's you, Sir.
ABSOLUTE	'has universally the character of being an accomplished gentleman, and a man of honour.' Well, that's handsome enough.
MRS MALAPROP	Oh, the fellow had some design in writing so –
ABSOLUTE	That he had, I'll answer for him, Ma'am.
MRS MALAPROP	But go on, Sir – you'll see presently.
ABSOLUTE	'As for the old weather-beaten she-dragon who guards you' – who can he mean by that?
MRS MALAPROP	*Me*, Sir – *me* – he means *me* there – what do you think now? But go on a little further.
ABSOLUTE	Impudent scoundrel! – 'it shall go hard but I will elude her vigilance, as I am told that the same ridiculous vanity, which makes her dress up her coarse features, and deck her dull chat with hard words which she don't understand –'
MRS MALAPROP	There, Sir! An attack upon my language! what do you think of that? An **aspersion** upon my parts of speech! Was ever such a brute! Sure if I **reprehend** anything in this world, it is the use of my **oracular** tongue, and a nice **derangement** of **epitaphs**!
ABSOLUTE	He deserves to be hanged and quartered! Let me see 'same ridiculous vanity –'
MRS MALAPROP	You need not read it again, Sir.
ABSOLUTE	I beg pardon, Ma'am – 'does also lay her open to the grossest deceptions from flattery and

---

aspersion insult.
reprehend arrest; but she means 'apprehend' (understand).
oracular to do with fortune-telling; she means 'vernacular' (from her own country).
derangement madness; she means 'arrangement'.
epitaphs words written on a gravestone; she means 'epigrams' (witty sayings).

pretended admiration' – an impudent coxcomb! 'so that I have a scheme to see you shortly with the old **harridan's** consent, and even to make her a go-between in our interviews.' – Was ever such assurance?

MRS MALAPROP Did you ever hear anything like it? He'll **elude my vigilance**, will he? Yes, yes! ha! ha! He's very likely to enter these doors – we'll try who can plot best.

---

harridan fierce old woman.
elude my vigilance get round my watchfulness.

Activities: Section A, Comedy

A1: Maid Marian and her Merry Men, page 2.

1   In groups of five (you will have to double up on some of the
    characters who don't say much), act out the extract.

    - Now talk about the characters and the relationships between
      them. For example, what kind of person is the Sheriff? Pick out
      things that he says which reveal his character. Who do you think
      are going to be the most important characters in this play? How
      can you tell?
    - After you have discussed these questions, act out the scene
      again and think about how you can emphasise the differences
      between the characters.

2   *Maid Marian and her Merry Men* is a comedy based on the
    traditional stories about Robin Hood.

    - The two Narrators and Barrington are like story-tellers. Think
      about the roles the Narrators play (including Barrington). Write
      down a) what the two Narrators tell us about what is happening
      on stage (such as who enters and what the set looks like); and
      b) what Barrington says which tells us what the main story-line
      will be.
    - In pairs, make a list of all the modern references (things from
      the twenty-first century that the playwright has included in his
      tale from the Middle Ages). These are called **anachronisms**:
      words and things which a writer places in the wrong period. Talk
      about the way in which Tony Robinson has used these
      anachronisms for comic effect.

3   Write a follow-up scene in which the Sheriff picks on someone else
    and victimises them. Try to write it in the style of Tony Robinson's
    play, with narrators. The opening speech by a narrator could be in
    rhyme, as Barrington's is, and the dialogue could include
    anachronisms.

A2: The Revengers' Comedies, page 5.

1   To gain an idea of the **visual comedy** – things that look funny – act
    out the scene in pairs. Henry will need a scarf and Karen a coat
    with a belt. A chair or two can represent the railings of the bridge.

    • After you have rehearsed the scene, perform it for another pair.

    • Decide what advice you would give to actors who were going to
      perform the scene, in order to make it funny.

2   Although both Henry and Karen seem to be about to throw
    themselves off a bridge, there are clues that they are pleased to
    have been prevented.

    • In pairs, re-read the extract and note down all the things which
      tell us that Henry and Karen don't really want to kill themselves,
      and that they would actually like to be befriended.

3   The scene after the one here is set in an all-night transport café.
    The stage direction reads '. . . *Faint jukebox music and the sound
    of an electronic game machine. Chatter from unseen lorry drivers.
    Henry appears carrying two very large mugs of tea . . .*'

    • Use the clues offered in the opening scene to write some
      dialogue for Karen and Henry in this second scene.

    • Compare your script with your partner's and support your ideas
      by referring to the extract.

    • Then discuss how you think the play will end.

A3: Twelfth Night, page 12.

1   Perform the scene in groups of three (Maria can also read the
    Servant's lines) and talk about how you might make a stage
    performance really funny. Think about:

    • Malvolio's actions (the script tells you some of the things he is
      doing, but you can add more)

- his tone of voice (how different is it from the way he usually speaks?)
- his costume – draw a sketch to show what he looks like.

Then freeze-frame the moments when a) he enters and Olivia sees him; b) he reacts to something Olivia says (for example, her suggestion 'Wilt thou go to bed, Malvolio?').

2 Most of the comedy in this situation is based on misunderstandings. Discuss the following questions in pairs:

- What does Malvolio believe, when he enters the room?
- What does Olivia come to think after a few seconds of conversation with him?
- In what ways does Malvolio completely misinterpret Olivia's instructions to Maria (lines 55–8). What does she mean by each of those statements and what does he think she means?

3 Write your own scene, in a modern setting, in which someone is suffering from a delusion like Malvolio's. Introduce the scene with a brief explanation of how the person came to be suffering from the misunderstanding (perhaps they are the victim of a practical joke, or have overheard something and misinterpreted it). Bring out the comedy that arises from the delusion.

A4: Red Dwarf, page 17.

1 In pairs, improvise a scene like the one between Rimmer and Lister. One of you (character A) has done something wrong and feels guilty about it, but is covering it up; the other one (character B) believes that A has done something really generous and is praising A for it. (For example, B might have broken a window at school. B thinks that A has taken the blame for it, while, in reality, A has informed the teacher that B did it.) Try to bring out B's pleasure and amazement, and A's guilt and embarrassment.

2   The various kinds of books or films with their own typical and recognisable features are called **genres**. Examples of common genres are: westerns, horror movies and spy thrillers. A **parody** is a comedy film or book which mocks or ridicules the typical features of a particular *genre*.

- In pairs, write down the features of a typical science fiction film set in deep space. (You could start the list with 'aliens' and 'amazingly advanced technology'.)
- Re-read the extract and list the features of the science fiction genre which are mocked in this parody. In each case, explain what the joke is.

Think about:

- the characters
- the situation they are in when the extract starts
- the technology
- the reference to Black Holes.

3   The comedy in this extract builds up, not only through the dialogue, but also through the series of shots that the viewer is given.

- Sketch (in rough outline only) ten frames of a storyboard to show the key moments at the climax of the episode. The first eight should be based on the stage directions at the opening of scenes 18 to 25. The ninth should show the moment where Lister re-enters and collects his guitar (7 lines from end); the tenth should show Rimmer peering through the guitar-shaped hole (last line).
- Finally, draw a frame showing the way the episode might end and write the accompanying dialogue.

A5: Loot, page 25.

1   To get a clear idea of the two characters' attitudes and behaviour, perform the scene without words. (In groups of three, one can play the body!) After you have rehearsed it a few times, discuss which

features of the script were a) easiest, and b) hardest to convey silently.

2   Is it right to link comedy and death in this way? Can you think of any other books, plays or films which do this?

3   Write director's notes to help the actors. In particular, how should the actor playing Dennis show his change of heart?

A6: Mak the Sheep-stealer, page 27.

1   In groups of five, make notes on the main things that happen in the scene.

   • Then improvise the whole scene, using your own words. Try to get across Mak's cunning, Gill's drunkenness, the shepherds' suspicion, their changing reactions to the 'baby' and Mak's desperation not to let them see into the cradle.

   Have fun with the bleating sounds of the sheep (which Gill tries to cover by groaning) and work out how to punish Mak at the end.

2   In the same groups, discuss the moments which you find funniest. It might be Gill groaning to cover the sheep's bleating, or the shepherds' discovery that the 'baby' 'is like to our sheep'. Discuss how you could get the humour across most successfully in a stage production.

3   The original play was written about eight centuries ago and, although this version by Tony Harrison was written in the 1980s, it keeps much of the 'flavour' of the Middle English language.

   • Use the footnotes to check the meanings of these words and phrases, which are not usually heard in modern Standard English:
     'I list well to eat'; 'ere it be slain';' 'I trow'

   • What phrases do the characters use instead of 'are you in?' (line 1) and 'Don't you see . . . ?' (line 3).

- Write your own version, in modern everyday English, of lines (70–9), where the shepherds return to the house and one of them discovers that the baby 'has a long snout'.

A7: Shakespeare in Love, page 34.

1   In groups of four, perform the opening scene in which Henslowe is tortured. Find a simple way to lower Henslowe's feet onto a mock fire, and make sure you bring out the differences between the characters. As you rehearse the scene, talk about Fennyman's responses to a) the fact that the new play is being written by Shakespeare; and b) the new play's title. What view does he take of Shakespeare? What kind of thing does Henslowe believe will appeal to the audience?

2   *Shakespeare in Love* is a screenplay: a script which has been written to be filmed, rather than performed on stage.

Now look at a couple of the TV scripts in this collection, for example, *Red Dwarf* and *Fawlty Towers*, which are also written to be filmed (for the small screen). Make a note of some differences between TV/film scripts and scripts written just for the stage, like Alan Ayckbourn's *Revengers' Comedies*.

Think about

- the stage directions
- the scene heads (which let you know where the scene is taking place)
- what can be done in a film or TV programme that can't be done on a stage in a theatre.

3   Write the opening page of a film screenplay in which somebody is lying to get out of a tricky situation. Sketch a couple of frames from the storyboard to give an idea of what the cinema audience will see.

A8: Educating Rita, page 39.

1   In pairs, re-read the scene and talk about the two characters.

    - What have you learned about Rita's background and her
      ambitions?
    - What kind of person is Frank?
    - Note down what you think are the main differences between
      them. Are there any similarities?

2   Rita's character comes across to the audience in a number of ways.
    One of the special things about her is her dialect. Pick out some
    examples of Rita's dialect which help to show how different she is
    from Frank. For example, look at the way she expresses

    - her excitement (lines 4–5 and 15–17);
    - her anxiety about the customer having a perm (lines 45–7;
      97–9).

3   Write a piece of dialogue between two people who come from very
    different backgrounds. You could decide to use Standard English
    dialect for one and a regional dialect for another.

A9: The Importance of Being Earnest, page 45.

1   Perform the scene in pairs. As you rehearse it, talk about a) the
    ways in which you can let the audience know about the differences
    in status between Jack and Lady Bracknell (who is the more
    powerful one); and b) the different tones of voice used by the two
    characters.

2   Lady Bracknell expresses some very strong opinions on a variety of
    matters. Many of them sound like proverbs. Write down what she
    says about:

    - smoking
    - how much a man should know before he gets married
    - education in England

- owning land
- where a 'simple, unspoiled' girl like Gwendolen ought to live
- losing both one's parents.

In pairs, discuss how each of these opinions is the opposite from what might be expected.

2 Write a scene in which one person wants another person to do something. The first, like Jack, has a problem; the second, like Lady Bracknell, is in a powerful position. Try to make the language of your second character a little like Lady Bracknell's – full of unexpected opinions, expressed like proverbs.

A10: Fawlty Towers, page 50.

1 The stage directions in this extract give a clear idea of the actions and precise movements the actors have to perform. Rehearse the scene in groups of six (someone can 'double' two of the smaller roles), paying attention to all the actions described in the stage directions.

2 A great deal of the comedy in this scene depends upon Manuel's limited understanding of English. In pairs, make a list of his mistakes with the language and discuss what the misunderstanding is in each case. For example, when Polly tries to help Manuel understand what 'a little sleep' means, she says 'siesta'. Thinking that this is the English word, Manuel replies 'Siesta . . . little sleep? . . . Same in Spanish.'

3 Write a short review of this extract, commenting on the comedy that is based upon a) visual jokes (such as Manuel holding the phone receiver out so that the caller can register that Basil is not there); and b) jokes based on the language (such as Manuel's misunderstandings).

A11: Pygmalion, page 58.

1   A performance of *Pygmalion* cannot be successful unless the
    actors get their accents exactly right.

    • Act out this extract in groups of six and practise giving the
      characters a very strong, upper-class Received Pronunciation
      accent.
    • Work hard on people's reactions to Eliza's speech: Higgins's
      when Eliza seems to be in danger of giving herself away;
      Freddie's to 'the new small talk'; and Pickering's to her final
      departing comment.

2   Although Eliza manages to put on a convincing accent, she still
    uses features of her London dialect.

    • Read Eliza's speeches out loud, starting at the point where she
      begins to talk about her aunt dying of influenza (line 43). (If you
      can manage different accents, it will help to read Eliza's
      speeches first in her upper-class accent, then in a London
      accent.)
    • Make a list of examples of Eliza's London dialect (such as 'they
      done the old woman in', line 45–6). Next to each example, write
      down what the Standard English version would have been.

3   Create a sketch in which someone disguises their usual style of
    language in order to pass themselves off as something else.
    Include a moment where they nearly give themselves away.

A12: The Rivals, page 63.

1   What do you think Mrs Malaprop should look like?

    • Perform her speeches and, in pairs, decide what sort of voice
      she ought to have, what mannerisms (such as gestures) and
      how she might move.
    • Decide which actress on television would be ideal for the part,
      in your opinion, and explain why.

2 Mrs Malaprop has given her name to a particular kind of mistake that people sometimes make when they speak. It is called a 'malapropism' and a good example is when Mrs Malaprop talks about the 'ineffectual' (useless) qualities in a woman, when she means 'intellectual' (to do with intelligence and thinking).

a) Use the footnotes to list Mrs Malaprop's malapropisms, together with the words she *meant* to use.

b) At another point in the play, she says: 'He can tell you the *perpendiculars*.' What did she mean to say?

c) Mrs Malaprop was by no means the first character in drama to use malapropisms. Shakespeare's Dogberry (a constable in *Much Ado About Nothing*) comes out with them all the time. What do you think he means by:

- You are thought here to be the most *senseless* and fit man for the constable of the watch . . .
- You shall *comprehend* all vagrom (homeless) men . . .
- to babble and to talk is most *tolerable* and not to be endured.

3 Write a short piece of dialogue involving Mrs Malaprop (or similar character, male or female), in which he or she uses malapropisms.

Section B: History

Although playwrights rely mainly on their imaginations, they sometimes choose to base their stories on real events from history. Often they do a great deal of research before beginning their writing. But it is important to remember that a history play is not the same as a factual history programme on television, which aims to report the known facts or discover new ones. The writer of a history play will usually have to invent the personalities of the characters or even change the details of events which are known to have happened. This is because their aim is to make us think, rather than teach us facts.

War has been a frequent subject for history plays through the ages, and the three extracts at the end of this section show some of the many ways in which it has been thought about and presented on stage.

B1: Our Country's Good

Writer: Timberlake Wertenbaker
Date: 1988
Staging: A set which can serve for a range of locations, from the hold of a convict ship to the Australian coast, to a settlement building.

The story so far

This is very near the opening of the play. The first scene is set in the hold of a convict ship bound for Australia in 1787. A prisoner is given fifty lashes and thrown into the hold with the others. The scene then switches to the coast of Australia.

ACT ONE

Scene One The Voyage Out

> *The hold of a convict ship bound for Australia, 1787. The convicts huddle together in the semi-darkness. On deck, the convict Robert Sideway is being flogged. Second Lieutenant Ralph Clark counts the lashes in a barely audible, slow and monotonous voice.*

RALPH CLARK Forty-four, forty-five, forty-six, forty-seven, forty-eight, forty-nine, fifty.

> *Sideway is untied and dumped with the rest of the convicts. He collapses. No one moves. A short silence.*

JOHN WISEHAMMER At night? The sea cracks against the ship. Fear whispers, screams, falls silent, hushed. Spewed from our country, forgotten, bound to the dark edge of the earth . . .

Scene Two A lone Aboriginal Australian describes the arrival of the First Convict Fleet in Botany Bay on January 20, 1788.

ABORIGINE   A giant canoe drifts onto the sea, clouds billowing from upright oars. This is a dream which has lost its way. Best to leave it alone.

Scene Three Punishment

Sydney Cove. Governor Arthur Phillip, Judge David Collins, Captain Watkin Tench, Midshipman Harry Brewer. The men are shooting birds.

PHILLIP   Was it necessary to cross fifteen thousand miles of ocean to erect another Tyburn?

TENCH   I should think it would make the convicts feel at home.

COLLINS   This land is under English law. The court found them guilty and sentenced them accordingly. There: a bald-eyed corella.

PHILLIP   But hanging?

COLLINS   Only the three who were found guilty of stealing from the colony's stores. And that, over there on the Eucalpytus, is a flock of 'cacatua galerita' – the sulphur-crested cockatoo. You have been made Governor-in-Chief of a paradise of birds, Arthur.

PHILLIP   And I hope not of a human hell, Davey. Don't shoot yet, Watkin, let's observe them. Could we not be more humane?

TENCH   Justice and humaneness have never gone hand in hand. The law is not a sentimental comedy.

PHILLIP   I am not suggesting they go without punishment. It is the spectacle of hanging I object to. The convicts

	will feel nothing has changed and will go back to their old ways.
TENCH	The convicts never left their old ways, Governor, nor do they intend to.
PHILLIP	Three months is not long enough to decide that. You're speaking too loud, Watkin.
COLLINS	I commend your endeavour to oppose the baneful influence of vice with the harmonising arts of civilisation, Governor, but I suspect your edifice will collapse without the mortar of fear.
PHILLIP	Have these men lost all fear of being flogged?
COLLINS	John Arscott has already been sentenced to 150 lashes for assault.
TENCH	The shoulder-blades are exposed at about 100 lashes and I would say that somewhere between 250 and 500 lashes you are probably condemning a man to death anyway.
COLLINS	With the disadvantage that the death is slow, unobserved and cannot serve as a sharp example.
PHILLIP	Harry?
HARRY	The convicts laugh at hangings, Sir. They watch them all the time.
TENCH	It's their favourite form of entertainment, I should say.
PHILLIP	Perhaps because they've never been offered anything else.
TENCH	Perhaps we should build an opera house for the convicts.
PHILLIP	We learned to love such things because they were offered to us when we were children or young men. Surely no one is born naturally cultured? I'll have the gun now.

COLLINS   We don't even have any books here, apart from the odd play and a few Bibles. And most of the convicts can't read so let us return to the matter in hand, which is the punishment of the convicts, not their education.

PHILLIP   Who are the condemned men, Harry?

HARRY   Thomas Barrett, age 17. Transported seven years for stealing one ewe sheep.

PHILLIP   Seventeen!

TENCH   It does seem to prove that the criminal tendency is innate.

PHILLIP   It proves nothing.

HARRY   James Freeman, age 25, Irish, transported fourteen years for assault on a sailor at Shadwell Dock.

COLLINS   I'm surprised he wasn't hanged in England.

HARRY   Handy Baker, marine and the thieves' ringleader.

COLLINS   He pleaded that it was wrong to put the convicts and the marines on the same rations and that he could not work on so little food. He almost swayed us.

TENCH   I do think that was an unfortunate decision. My men are in a ferment of discontent.

COLLINS   Our Governor-in-Chief would say it is justice, Tench, and so it is. It is also justice to hang these men.

TENCH   The sooner the better, I believe. There is much excitement in the colony about the hangings. It's their theatre, Governor, you cannot change that.

PHILLIP   I would prefer them to see real plays: fine language, sentiment.

TENCH   No doubt Garrick would relish the prospect of eight months at sea for the pleasure of entertaining a group of criminals and the odd savage.

PHILLIP	I never liked Garrick, I always preferred Macklin.
COLLINS	I'm a Kemble man myself. We will need a hangman.
PHILLIP	Harry, you will have to organise the hanging and eventually find someone who agrees to fill that hideous office.

Phillip shoots.

COLLINS	Shot.
TENCH	Shot.
HARRY	Shot, Sir.
COLLINS	It is my belief the hangings should take place tomorrow. The quick execution of justice for the good of the colony, Governor.
PHILLIP	The good of the colony? Oh, look! We've frightened a kankaroo.

They look

ALL	Ah!
HARRY	There is also Dorothy Handland, 82, who stole a biscuit from Robert Sideway.
PHILLIP	Surely we don't have to hang an 82-year-old woman?
COLLINS	That will be unnecessary. She hanged herself this morning.

Scene Four The Loneliness of Men

Ralph Clark's tent. It is late at night. Ralph stands, composing and speaking his diary.

B2: Journey's End

Writer: R.C. Sherriff
Date: 1928
Staging: The whole play takes place in a British dug-out during the Great War, March 1918. R.C. Sherriff's stage directions are very clear and detailed:

'A few rough steps lead into the trench, above, through a low doorway. A table occupies a good space of the dug-out floor. A wooden frame, covered with wire netting, stands against the left wall and serves the double purpose of a bed and a seat for the table. A wooden bench against the back wall makes another seat, and two boxes serve for the other sides.

Another wire-covered bed is fixed in the right corner beyond the doorway.

Gloomy tunnels lead out of the dug-out to left and right.

Except for the table, beds and seats, there is no furniture save the bottles holding the candles, and a few tattered magazine pictures pinned to the wall of girls in flimsy costumes.

The earth walls deaden the sounds of war, making them faint and far away, although the front line is only fifty yards ahead. The flames of the candles that burn day and night are steady in the still, damp air.'

The story so far
Osborne, the oldest officer in the dug-out, and Raleigh, an eighteen-year-old who has only just arrived from England, have been chosen to lead a raid into the enemy trenches. They wait for the order.

        There is silence in the dug-out. Osborne has been filling his pipe, and stands lighting it as Raleigh returns.

OSBORNE   Just time for a small pipe.

RALEIGH   Good. I'll have a cigarette, I think. *(He feels in his pocket.)*

OSBORNE   Here you are. *(He offers his case to Raleigh.)*

RALEIGH	I say, I'm always smoking yours.
OSBORNE	That's all right. *(Pause.)* What about this coffee?
RALEIGH	Sure.

They sit at the table.

OSBORNE	Are you going to have a drop of rum in it?
RALEIGH	Don't you think it might make us a – a bit muzzy?
OSBORNE	I'm just having the coffee as it is.
RALEIGH	I think I will, too.
OSBORNE	We'll have the rum afterwards – to celebrate.
RALEIGH	That's a much better idea.

They stir their coffee in silence. Osborne's eyes meet Raleigh's. He smiles.

OSBORNE	How d'you feel?
RALEIGH	All right.
OSBORNE	I've got a sort of empty feeling inside.
RALEIGH	That's just what I've got!
OSBORNE	Wind up!
RALEIGH	I keep wanting to yawn.
OSBORNE	That's it. Wind up. I keep wanting to yawn too. It'll pass off directly we start.
RALEIGH	*(taking a deep breath)* I wish we could go now.
OSBORNE	*(looking at his watch on the table)* We've got eight minutes yet.
RALEIGH	Oh, Lord!
OSBORNE	Let's just have a last look at the map. *(He picks up the map and spreads it out.)* Directly the smoke's thick enough, I'll give the word. You run straight for this point here –
RALEIGH	When I get to the Boche wire I lie down and wait for you.

OSBORNE	Don't forget to throw your bombs.
RALEIGH	*(patting his pocket)* No. I've got them here.
OSBORNE	When I shout 'Righto!' – in you go with your eight men. I shall lie on the Boche parapet, and blow my whistle now and then to show you where I am. Pounce on the first Boche you see and bundle him out to me.
RALEIGH	Righto.
OSBORNE	Then we come back like blazes.
RALEIGH	The whole thing'll be over quite quickly?
OSBORNE	I reckon with luck we shall be back in three minutes.
RALEIGH	As quick as that?
OSBORNE	I think so. *(He folds up the map.)* And now let's forget all about it for – *(He looks at his watch.)* – for six minutes.
RALEIGH	Oh, Lord, I can't!
OSBORNE	You must.
RALEIGH	How topping if we both get the M.C.!
OSBORNE	Yes. *(Pause.)* Your coffee sweet enough?
RALEIGH	Yes, thanks. It's jolly good coffee. *(Pause.)* I wonder what the Boche are doing over there now?
OSBORNE	I don't know. D'you like coffee better than tea?
RALEIGH	I do for breakfast. *(Pause.)* Do these smoke bombs make much row when they burst?
OSBORNE	Not much. *(Pause.)* Personally, I like cocoa for breakfast.
RALEIGH	*(laughing)* I'm sorry!
OSBORNE	Why sorry? Why shouldn't I have cocoa for breakfast?
RALEIGH	I don't mean that. I – mean – I'm sorry to keep talking about the raid. It's so difficult to – to talk about anything else. I was just wondering – will the Boche retaliate in any way after the raid?

OSBORNE	Bound to – a bit.
RALEIGH	Shelling?
OSBORNE	'The time has come,' the Walrus said, 'To talk of many things: Of shoes – and ships – and sealing wax – Of cabbages – and kings.'
RALEIGH	'And why the sea is boiling hot– And whether pigs have wings.'
OSBORNE	Now we're off! Quick, let's talk about pigs! Black pigs or white pigs!
RALEIGH	Black pigs. In the New Forest you find them, quite wild.
OSBORNE	You know the New Forest?
RALEIGH	Rather! My home's down there. A little place called Allum Green, just outside Lyndhurst.
OSBORNE	I know Lyndhurst well.
RALEIGH	It's rather nice down there.
OSBORNE	I like it more than any place I know.
RALEIGH	I think I do, too. Of course, it's different when you've always lived in a place.
OSBORNE	You like it in a different way.
RALEIGH	Yes. Just behind our house there's a stream called the Highland; it runs for miles – right through the middle of the forest. Dennis and I followed it once as far as we could.
OSBORNE	I used to walk a lot round Lyndhurst.
RALEIGH	I wish we'd known each other then. You could have come with Dennis and me.
OSBORNE	I wish I had. I used to walk alone.
RALEIGH	You must come and stay with us one day.
OSBORNE	I should like to – awfully.

RALEIGH   I can show you places in the forest that nobody knows about except Dennis and me. It gets thicker and darker and cooler, and you stir up all kinds of funny wild animals.

OSBORNE   They say there are ruins, somewhere in the forest, of villages that William the Conqueror pulled down to let the forest grow.

RALEIGH   I know. We often used to look for them, but we haven't found them yet. *(Pause.)* You must come and help look one day.

OSBORNE   I'll find them all right.

RALEIGH   Then you can write to the papers. 'Dramatic Discovery of Professor Osborne!'

Osborne laughs.

OSBORNE   I did go exploring once – digging up Roman remains.

RALEIGH   Where was that?

OSBORNE   Near my home in Sussex there's a Roman road called Stane Street; it runs as straight as a line from the coast to London.

RALEIGH   I know it.

OSBORNE   Near where I live the road runs over Bignor Hill, but in recent times a new road's been cut round the foot of the hill, meeting the old road again farther on. The old road over the hill hasn't been used for years and years – and it's all grown over with grass, and bushes and trees grow in the middle of it.

RALEIGH   Can you still see where it runs?

OSBORNE   Quite easily, in places.

RALEIGH   Did you dig a bit of it up, then?

OSBORNE   Yes. We got permission to dig out a section. It was in wonderful condition.

RALEIGH	Did you find anything?
OSBORNE	We found a horseshoe – and a Roman penny.
RALEIGH	*(laughing)* Splendid!
OSBORNE	It's awfully fascinating, digging like that.
RALEIGH	It must be.

Osborne glances at his watch.

	Is it time yet?
OSBORNE	Two minutes. Then we must go up. I wish we had a good hot bath waiting for us when we get back.
RALEIGH	So do I. *(Pause.)* We're having something special for dinner, aren't we?
OSBORNE	How did you know? It's supposed to be a secret.
RALEIGH	Mason dropped a hint.
OSBORNE	Well, we've had a fresh chicken sent up from Noyelle Farm.
RALEIGH	I say!
OSBORNE	And a most awful luxury – two bottles of champagne and half a dozen cigars! One each and one spare one in case one explodes.
RALEIGH	I've never smoked a cigar.
OSBORNE	It's bound to make you sick.

Raleigh notices Osborne's ring on the table; he picks it up.

RALEIGH	I say, here's your ring.
OSBORNE	Yes. I'm I'm leaving it here. I don't want the risk of losing it.
RALEIGH	Oh! *(There is silence. He puts the ring slowly down.)*
OSBORNE	*(rising)* Well, I think perhaps we ought to get ready.
RALEIGH	Yes. Righto. *(He also rises.)*

OSBORNE	I'm not going to wear a belt – just my revolver, with the lanyard round my neck.
RALEIGH	I see. *(He puts his lanyard round his neck and grips his revolver.)* I feel better with this in my hand, don't you?
OSBORNE	Yes. Something to hold. Loaded all right?
RALEIGH	Yes.

They put on their helmets. Osborne takes his pipe from his mouth and lays it carefully on the table.

OSBORNE	I do hate leaving a pipe when it's got a nice glow on the top like that.
RALEIGH	*(with a short laugh)* What a pity!

There is another pause. Osborne glances at his watch as it lies on the table.

OSBORNE	Three minutes to. I think we'd better go.
RALEIGH	Righto.

Their eyes meet as Osborne turns from the table.

OSBORNE	I'm glad it's you and I – together, Raleigh.
RALEIGH	*(eagerly)* Are you – really?
OSBORNE	Yes.
RALEIGH	So am I – awfully.
OSBORNE	We must put up a good show.
RALEIGH	Yes. Rather!

There is a short pause.

OSBORNE	Let's go along, shall we?
RALEIGH	Righto.

They go towards the steps.

B3: Blackadder Goes Forth

Writers: Richard Curtis and Ben Elton
Date: 1998
Staging: Television.
The story so far

This extract is from the end of the final episode. As is usual for the series, Colonel Melchett is at Headquarters, supported by Captain Darling, while Blackadder, George and Baldrick are in their front-line trench. News has come that the big attack is scheduled for tomorrow. Blackadder is not the only one who is keen to avoid it . . .

Scene 3 Melchett's HQ

The lights are on very low. Melchett comes in wearing a dressing gown and a beautiful hair-net over his moustache. Darling has dozed off at the desk.

MELCHETT   Darling!

Darling jumps up at the sound of his voice.

DARLING   Sir.

MELCHETT   Can't sleep either, eh?

DARLING   No, sir. Thinking about the push, sir. Hoping the Boche'll forget to set their alarm clocks, oversleep and still be in their pyjamas when our boys turn up, sir.

MELCHETT   Yes, yes. I've been thinking, too. Darling . . .

DARLING   Sir?

MELCHETT   You know – over these last years. I've come to think of you as a sort of son. Not a favourite son, of course – Lord no! – more a sort of illegitimate, backstairs sort of sprog. You know, the sort of spotty squit you never really like – but still fruit of my overactive loins.

DARLING   Thank you, sir.

MELCHETT   And I want to do what's best for you, Darling. So I've thought about it a great deal and I want you to have this . . .

He hands him a piece of paper.

DARLING   *(trying to look pleased)* A postal order for ten shillings.

MELCHETT   Ah – no – sorry. My godson's wedding present.

He hands over another piece of paper.

DARLING   Ah, no, sir – this is a commission for the front line, sir.

He tries to hand it back.

MELCHETT   Yes. I've been awfully selfish keeping you back here instead of letting you join in all the fun and games. This will let you get to the front line immediately.

DARLING   But, sir – I don't want to . . .

MELCHETT   To leave me? I appreciate that, Darling. But dammit – I'll just have to enter Berlin without someone to carry my special feathery hat.

DARLING   No, sir – I don't want to go into battle . . .

Melchett won't let Darling finish his sentences.

MELCHETT   . . . without me? I know. But I'm too old. I'll just have to sit this one out on the touchline with the half-time oranges and the fat wheezy boys with a note from matron, while you young bloods link arms for the glorious final scrum down.

Darling stands up, and comes round next to General Melchett.

DARLING   You're not listening, sir, I'm begging – please, for the sake of all the times I've helped you with your dickie bows and your dicky bladder, please . . .

He falls on his knees in front of the General.

. . . don't make me . . .

MELCHETT   *(patting him reassuringly on the head)* . . . go through the farewell debagging ceremony in the mess? No, I've spared you that, you touchingly sentimental young booby. Look – no fuss, no bother – the driver is already here.

The door opens. Light floods in, shining on Darling's face. A big shadow appears at the door, and he turns round, still on his knees, to face it.

DARLING   But . . .

MELCHETT   No, not a word. Believe me, Kevin, I know what you want to say, I know.

Melchett stands.

Goodbye, Kevin Darling.

He salutes.

DARLING   Goodbye, sir.

He salutes and walks sadly to the door.

Scene 4 The dug-out, the trench and Field Marshal Haig's staff HQ

It's dawn and becoming a little lighter. Blackadder has his coat and hat on, and is ready to go. Baldrick is looking out of the dug-out flap.

BALDRICK	It's stopped raining at last, begging your pardon, sir. Looks like we might have a nice day for it.

George goes to the dug-out entrance.

GEORGE	Yes, it's nearly morning . . .
BLACKADDER	Good Lord, so it is – time to make my call *(He dials breezily. It answers.)* Hello. Field Marshal Sir Douglas Haig, please. Yes, it's urgent.

Haig is standing in his very opulent office, in front of a battle reconstruction with lots of tiny model soldiers.

HAIG	Haig.
BLACKADDER	Hello, Sir Douglas.
HAIG	Who is this?
BLACKADDER	This is Captain Blackadder, sir. Erstwhile of the 19/45th East African Rifles.
HAIG	Good Lord! Blackie!

He knocks over one set of soldiers with a deft sweep of the hand.

BLACKADDER	Yes, sir.
HAIG	*(knocking over another set)* By heaven. Blackie – I haven't seen you since . . .
BLACKADDER	'92, sir, Mboto Gorge.
HAIG	By jingo, yes. We sure gave those pigmies a good squashing.
BLACKADDER	Certainly did, sir. And do you remember . . .
HAIG	My God, yes – you saved my damn life that day, Blackie. If it weren't for you, that pigmy woman with the sharpened mango could have seriously . . .
BLACKADDER	Well, yes, sir. And do you remember you said then that if I was ever in real trouble, if I ever really

needed a favour, I was to call you and you'd do anything you could to help me?

HAIG Yes, yes I do. And I stick by it. You know me, not a man to change my mind.

He starts sweeping up the toy soldiers with a dustpan and brush.

BLACKADDER No, we've noticed that.

HAIG So, what do you want? Spit it out, man.

He chucks the dustpan's contents over his shoulder.

BLACKADDER Well, sir, it's like this. I'll be blunt. It's the big push today and I'm not *all that* keen to go over the top.

HAIG *(not happy)* Ah. Oh, I see. Well . . .

He sits down.

BLACKADDER *(casually)* It was a viciously sharp mango slice, wasn't it, sir . . .

HAIG Well, this is most irregular, but, all right. But if I fix it for you I never want to hear from you again, is that clear?

He picks up one of the toy soldiers he's knocked over and sets it upright.

BLACKADDER Suits me, Duggie.

HAIG Very well, listen carefully, Blackadder. I won't repeat this. Right – first put your underpants on your head, and two pencils up your nose. They'll think you're crazy and send you home. Right, favour returned.

He hangs up. Blackadder is not amused.

BLACKADDER I think the phrase rhymes with 'clucking bell'.

BALDRICK	Does that mean that you're going to have to go over the top now?
	Blackadder nods. Phone rings. Blackadder leaps on it.
BLACKADDER	Field Marshal!
MELCHETT	*(at his HQ)* Ha! Ha! No – not quite. Or not yet. Blackadder, wanted to let you know I've sent a little surprise over for you.
	Darling appears framed in the door of the trench in fighting gear.
GEORGE	Sir.
BLACKADDER	Captain Darling.
	He puts down the phone. They stare at each other, knowing what it means for both of them.
DARLING	Captain Blackadder.
BLACKADDER	Here to join us for the last waltz?
DARLING	Ahm – yes, that's right – tired of folding the general's pyjamas.
GEORGE	Well, this is splendid comradely news! Together we'll fight for king and country and be sucking sausages in Berlin by teatime . . .
BLACKADDER	Yes. I hope the cafés are well stocked. Everyone seems determined to eat out the moment they arrive.
GEORGE	But really this is brave, splendid, and noble . . .
	Blackadder doesn't react. Long pause as all four stand together.
	Sir.
BLACKADDER	Yes, Lieutenant.

GEORGE	I'm scared, sir.
BALDRICK	I'm scared too, sir.
GEORGE	I'm the last of the tiddly-winking leapfroggers from the golden summer of 1914. I don't want to die . . . I'm really not over keen on dying at all, sir.
BLACKADDER	How are you feeling. Darling?
DARLING	Ahm – not all that good, Blackadder. Rather hoped I'd get through the whole show, go back to work at Pratt and Sons, keep wicket for the Croydon Gentlemen, marry Doris. Made a note in my diary on the way here. Simply says: 'Bugger'.
BLACKADDER	Well, quite.

Outside is heard the muffled faraway cry: ' Stand to, stand to, fix bayonets!'

Come on, come on, let's move.

They all move out. At the door, Blackadder turns to George.

Don't forget your stick, Lieutenant.

GEORGE	*(picking up his stick)* Rather, sir. Wouldn't want to face a machine-gun without this.

They emerge in the misty trenches and all stand in a line, ready for the off. Then suddenly there is a silence. The machine guns stop.

DARLING	I say, listen – our guns have stopped.
GEORGE	You don't think . . .
BALDRICK	Perhaps the war's over. Perhaps it's peace.
GEORGE	Hurrah! The big nobs have got round a table and yanked the iron out of the fire.
DARLING	Thank God – we lived through it – The Great War, 1914 to 1917.

ALL THREE	Hip, hip hurray!!!
BLACKADDER	I'm afraid not. The guns have stopped because we are about to attack. Not even our generals are mad enough to shell their own men. They feel it's more sporting to let the Germans do it.
GEORGE	So, we are, in fact, going over. This is, as they say, it?
BLACKADDER	Yes, unless I can think of something very quickly.

A command is heard: 'Company, one pace forward.' They all take one step forward.

| BALDRICK | There's a nasty splinter on that ladder, sir. A bloke could hurt himself on that. |

A call: 'Stand ready.' They put their hands on the ladders, ready to climb over.

I have a plan, sir.

BLACKADDER	Really, Baldrick, a cunning and subtle one?
BALDRICK	Yes, sir.
BLACKADDER	As cunning as a fox who's just been appointed Professor of Cunning at Oxford University.
BALDRICK	Yes, sir.

Another call is heard: 'On the signal, Company will advance.'

| BLACKADDER | Well, I'm afraid it's too late. Whatever it was, I'm sure it was better than my plan to get out of this by pretending to be mad. I mean, who would have noticed another madman round here? |

A whistle goes. He looks at Baldrick.

Good luck, everyone.

Blackadder blows his whistle. There is a roar of voices – everyone leaps up the ladders. As they rise above the sandbags they are met by thunderous machine-gun fire.

Blackadder, Baldrick, George and Darling run on, brandishing their hand-guns. They will not get far.

Silence falls. Our soldiers fade away. No Man's Land turns slowly into a peaceful field of poppies. The only sound is that of a bird, singing sweetly.

B4: Henry V

Writer: William Shakespeare
Date: 1599
Staging: *Henry V* might have been one of the first plays to be acted in the new Globe playhouse. If not, its first performance would have been in the Curtain, north of the Thames, another amphitheatre playhouse.

The story so far

In pursuit of his claim to the French crown, King Henry V has crossed the English Channel with his army and is attacking the town of Harfleur. Among the soldiers who make up his troops are several characters who led a riotous life with Henry before he became King: Pistol, Bardolph and Nym. As the scene opens, Henry is urging his men to make one more attack through the gap that has been made in the town's defences.

ACT III

Scene 1

Alarum. Enter Soldiers with scaling-ladders at Harfleur.
Enter the King, Exeter, Bedford and Gloucester.

KING   Once more unto the **breach**, dear friends, once more,
    Or close the wall up with our English dead.
    In peace there's nothing **so becomes** a man
    As modest stillness and humility;
    But when the blast of war blows in our ears,
    Then imitate the action of the tiger:
    Stiffen the sinews, conjure up the blood

---

breach hole in the defences.
so becomes is more appropriate for.
Stiffen the sinews tense your muscles.
conjure up the blood get the blood coursing through your veins.

Disguise fair nature with hard-favoured rage.
Then lend the eye a terrible aspect;
Let it pry through the portage of the head   10
Like the brass cannon; let the brow o'erwhelm it
As fearfully as doth a galled rock
O'erhang and jutty his confounded base,
Swilled with the wild and wasteful ocean.
Now set the teeth and stretch the nostril wide,
Hold hard the breath and bend up every spirit
To his full height. On, on, you noble English,
Whose blood is fet from fathers of war-proof,
Fathers that like so many Alexanders
Have in these parts from morn till even fought,   20
And sheathed their swords for lack of argument.
Dishonour not your mothers; now attest
That those whom you called fathers did beget you.
Be copy now to men of grosser blood
And teach them how to war. And you, good yeomen,
Whose limbs were made in England, show us here
The mettle of your pasture; let us swear
That you are worth your breeding – which I doubt not,
For there is none of you so mean and base.
That hath not noble lustre in your eyes.   30

Disguise fair nature Hide your usually kind looks.
Then lend . . . have a terrible look in your eyes.
portage portholes.
bend up strain to the utmost.
fet derived.
of war-proof who have proved themselves in war.
for lack of argument when there was no one left to fight.
Dishonour not Don't bring disgrace upon your mothers.
attest . . . **you** prove that the men you call your fathers actually were.
Be copy . . . **blood** be an example to the men who are not nobles.
yeomen farmers.
show . . . **pasture** prove how good your upbringing has been.
noble lustre the gleam of nobility.

I see you stand like greyhounds in the **slips**,
Straining upon the start. The game's afoot.
Follow your spirit, and **upon this charge**
Cry 'God for Harry! England and Saint George!'

[Exeunt.] Alarum, and chambers go off.

Scene 2

Enter Nym, Bardolph, Pistol and Boy.

BARDOLPH   On, on, on, on, on, to the breach, to the breach!

NYM   Pray thee, Corporal, stay; **the knocks are too hot**, and
for mine own part I have not a case of lives. **The
humour of it** is too hot, that is the **very plain-song** of it.

PISTOL   The plain-song is most just, for **humours** do abound.
Knocks go and come, God's **vassals** drop and die,
　　　And sword and shield
　　　In bloody field
　　　Doth win immortal fame.   10

BOY   **Would I were** in an alehouse in London! I would give
all my fame for a pot of ale and safety.

PISTOL   And I.
　　　If wishes would **prevail** with me
　　　 My purpose should not fail with me,
　　　But **thither would I hie**.

---

slips leashes
upon this charge as you charge or, on my word of command.
the knocks . . . hot it's too dangerous.
The humour of it that's the way it's going.
very plain-song simple plain truth.
humours bad temper.
vassals servants.
Would I were I wish I were.
prevail come true.
thither . . . hie that's where I would rush to.

BOY	As duly –
	But not as truly
	As bird doth sing on bough.

Enter Fluellen.

FLUELLEN	*(beats them)* Up to the breach, you dogs! **Avaunt,**	20
	you cullions!	

PISTOL	Be merciful, great duke, to **men of mould!**
	Abate they rage, abate thy manly rage,
	Abate thy rage, great duke!
	Good **bawcock**, bate thy rage! **Use lenity**, sweet
	chuck!

NYM	**These be good humours!** Your honour runs bad
	humours!

Exeunt all but Boy.

Avaunt, you cullions! Go, on, you scum!
men of mould mortal men.
Abate stop.
bawcock . . . chuck (affectionate terms)
Use lenity be lenient.
These . . . humours This is a fine way to behave!

Activities: Section B, History

B1: Our Country's Good, page 80.

1   The tension in this extract builds up, not only through the
    dialogue, but also through the sequence of scenes one after
    another.

    - Sketch (in rough outline only) six frames of a storyboard to
      show the key moments in these opening scenes. Use the
      opening stage directions to each scene as a basis for four of the
      frames.
    - Now compare your drawings with a partner and discuss what
      the audience learns about the play from these opening
      moments.

2   Re-read Scene 3. What does the dialogue tell us about Phillip,
    Collins and Tench?

    - For example, what different views do they take about the
      effectiveness of hanging and the ways in which the convicts
      ought to be treated?
    - In what ways are the men similar? (Think about their attitudes
      to the theatre and the Australian wildlife, for example.)

3   As Scene 4 opens, Second Lieutenant Ralph Clark (who appeared
    in Scene 1) is writing his diary, having been at a meal with
    Governor Phillip and others. Write his diary entry, in which he
    comments on a) the flogging of the convict on board ship; b) his
    first impressions of Australia, including the Aboriginal Australians
    and the wildlife; and c) his views on the hangings.

B2: Journey's End, page 85.

1   In pairs, pick a section from this extract and rehearse it. Try to convey to an audience a) the friendship between the two soldiers; b) the anxiety and tension. Look, for example, at the moment when Raleigh reminds Osborne that he has left his ring on the table. How will you show that, beneath their matter-of-fact conversation, they are both frightened?

2   How would you know that this play was set in a period in the past? Pick out some of the expressions used by Raleigh and Osborne which you would not hear today and write down their modern equivalents. For example, what might an excited eighteen year-old say instead of 'How topping . . . '?

3   R.C. Sherriff cleverly builds the tension in this scene by dividing it up into different phases: smoking and drinking coffee; checking the map and their plan; Osborne's attempts to take Raleigh's mind off the raid (including planning future visits to the New Forest and talking about archaeology); discussing that evening's meal; making final preparations.

   • Write a short account to show how he builds the tension, commenting on the different phases and what happens in each one. Conclude by saying how we feel at the end of the scene. Do we expect either of the men to come back, for example, and why?

B3: Blackadder Goes Forth, page 92.

1   In pairs, act out Scene 3. Show Darling's desperation not to be sent to the front line, and Melchett's complete refusal to listen.

2   This sequence of scenes contains several different kinds of humour. In pairs, talk about the ways in which the writers have used:
   • comedy based on the situation (e.g. Scene 3)
   • visual comedy (e.g. Haig and the toy soldiers)

- comedy which comes from the language (e.g. Baldrick saying 'Looks like we might have a nice day for it')
- 'dark' comedy (e.g. Baldrick warning Blackadder to mind the 'nasty splinter').

3   Although *Blackadder Goes Forth* is a comedy, it undoubtedly has a serious side to it. Write an account of this final sequence of the final episode, bringing out a) the features of the story and setting which are based solidly on historical facts; b) the different kinds of comedy (see question 2); and c) the serious elements (where does the tone suddenly become serious?).

B4: Henry V, page 101.

1   In groups of six, take it in turns to perform Henry's speech in Scene 1, making it as stirring and heroic as you can.

- Now perform it again, this time adding Scene 2 – Pistol, Bardolph and Nym's attempt to run away. Make them as cowardly and as reluctant to fight as you possibly can.
- Talk about the difference between the first performance and the second. What effect does Scene 2 have? Why is it there?

2   All Shakespeare's verse has a pattern of light and heavy stresses running through it, called the **metre.** You can hear the metre if you read the following line out loud, over-emphasising the stressed syllables:

But **when** the **blast** of **war** blows **in** our **ears** (line 5)

You would not want to perform the line like that, because it would sound boring, but the metre is always there, as a kind of underlying rhythm, like the beat in music.

Look at line 5 again. It can be divided into five sections, like musical bars. They are called **feet:**

But **when** I the **blast** I of **war** I blows **in** I our **ears**

Verse which contains lines made up of five feet is called **pentameter** (*pent* comes from the Greek word for five). A foot of two syllables in which the stress falls on the second syllable is called an **iamb**. So Shakespeare's verse is called iambic pentameter.

- Find the following lines and read them out loud. Then pick five, copy them out and mark in a) the heavy stresses; and b) the divisions into five feet:

  lines 1, 15, 21, 22, 24, 26, 27, 30, 31, 34.

3 Imagine you are a radio journalist and write a commentary on the two scenes. Say things about Henry's heroic speech and then add a commentary on what Pistol, Bardolph and Nym do.

- Give your opinions on how successful Henry's speech has been in stirring up his troops for a final attack.
- Finally, perform the commentary, recording it if you can, with other people acting the Shakespeare dialogue in the background and providing sound effects.

Section C: Tragedy

A tragedy is a play which shows how a happy and successful person suffers a great disaster and usually meets their death by the end of the drama.

The first tragedies were written two and a half thousand years ago in ancient Greece – there is an example of one in this section – and reached a high point in this country with the great tragedies of writers such as Christopher Marlowe and William Shakespeare in the time of Queen Elizabeth I and James I.

The extracts in this section have been chosen, not only because they are from exciting and famous plays, but because they represent four different ways in which tragedy can come about:

- In Æschylus's play, King Agamemnon's tragedy begins with a terrible mistake – his decision to sacrifice his daughter;
- Faustus's tragedy happens because of a personal flaw or weakness – his lust for knowledge and power;
- Romeo and Juliet seem to be the tragic victims of a cruel fate;
- Hamlet's tragedy is set in motion when the ghost of his dead father appears and commands him to avenge his death.

C1: The Agamemnon

Writer: Æschylus (this modern translation was written by Phillip Vellacott in 1956)

Date: around 480 BCE

Staging: open amphitheatre with a circular stage and a building behind it (the *skene*, which gives us the word *scene*)

The story so far

Ten years before this story begins, the Greek King Agamemnon (pronounced *Agger-**mem**-non*) had summoned a great fleet together. Its aim was to sail to Troy and recapture Helen, the wife of Agamemnon's brother, Menelaus (*Menner-**lay**-us*), who had been stolen away by the Trojan Prince Paris. The fleet gathered and were ready to set sail when suddenly the wind dropped. The priests told Agamemnon that the goddess Artemis was angry with him and that, to appease her, he would have to sacrifice his young daughter, Iphigenia (*Iffy-**gain**-ia*). In this scene near the beginning of the play, a group of city elders – wise old men of Argos – tell the audience what then took place. This group is known as the 'chorus': people whose job it is to set the scene for us, fill in parts of the story and comment on what happens.

The elder king then spoke: 'What can I say?
Disaster follows if I disobey;
Surely yet worse disaster if I yield
And slaughter my own child, my home's delight,
In her young innocence, and stain my hand
With **blasphemous** unnatural cruelty,
Bathed in the blood I fathered! Either way,
Ruin! Disband the fleet, sail home, and earn
The deserter's badge – abandon my command,

The elder king King Agamemnon, senior to his brother Menelaus.
blasphemous against the gods.

Betray the alliance – now? The wind must turn,
There must be sacrifice, a maid must bleed –
Their **chafing rage** demands it – they are right!
May good **prevail**, and justify my deed!'

Then he put on
The harness of Necessity.
The doubtful tempest of his soul
Veered, and his prayer was turned to blasphemy,
His offering to **impiety**.
Hence that **repentance** late and long
Which, since his madness passed, **pays toll**
For that one reckless wrong.
Shameless self-willed infatuation
Emboldens men to dare damnation,
And starts the wheels of doom which roll
Relentless to their piteous **goal**.

So Agamemnon, rather than retreat,
Endured to offer up his daughter's life
To help a war fought for **a faithless wife**
And pay the ransom for a storm-bound fleet.

Heedless of her tears,
Her cries of 'Father!' and her maiden years,

---

chafing rage violent anger.
prevail be victorious.
Then he put . . . Necessity a way of saying: 'He did what had to be done.'
Veered switched this way and that.
impiety unholy wickedness.
repentance regret; desire to put things right.
pays toll Agamemnon has had to pay heavily for this one mad mistake
Shameless . . . goal Stubborn pride and self-love can lead men to commit damnable
deeds, and start a train of events in motion which will lead them to their pitiful doom.
a faithless wife the Greek Helen, wife of Menelaus, who had run off with the Trojan
prince, Paris.

Her judges valued more
Their glory and their war.
A prayer was said. Her father gave the word.
Limp in her flowing dress
The priest's attendants held her high
Above the altar, as men hold a **kid**.
Her father spoke again, to bid
One bring a gag, and press
Her sweet mouth tightly with a cord,
Lest **Atreus' house** be cursed by some **ill-omened** cry.

Rough hands tear at her girdle, cast
Her **saffron** silks to earth. Her eyes
Search for her slaughterers; and each,
Seeing her beauty, that surpassed
A painter's vision, yet denies
The pity her dumb looks **beseech**,
Struggling for voice; for often in old days,
When brave men feasted in her father's hall,
With simple skill and **pious** praise
Linked to the flute's pure tone
Her virgin voice would melt the hearts of all,
Honouring the third **libation** near her father's throne.

The rest I did not see,
Nor do I speak of it . . .
                              But this I know:

---

kid young goat (to be sacrificed).
Atreus' house Agamemnon's family (Atreus was his father).
ill-omened bringing bad luck.
saffron dyed yellow.
beseech beg for.
pious religious.
libation drink offered up to the gods.

What **Calchas** prophesies will be fulfilled.
The scale of Justice falls **in equity**:
The killer will be killed.

Calchas the priest.
in equity evenly; fairly.

C2: Doctor Faustus

Writer: Christopher Marlowe
Date: around 1592
Staging: It was probably first performed in The Rose playhouse on Bankside, a building like Shakespeare's Globe (and quite close to it), but slightly smaller. The foundations of The Rose were uncovered a few years ago and can still be seen.

The story so far

The brilliant Doctor John Faustus has excelled in every area of human knowledge, but still he wants to know more and, against the advice of all his friends, has begun to explore the possibilities of black magic. In this scene, he conjures up the devil Mephostophilis (*Meffo-**stof**-fillis*) and offers to sell his soul, if the devil will do what he commands.

Scene 5

> . . . What power can hurt me? Faustus, thou art safe:
> **Cast** no more doubts! Mephostophilis, come,
> And bring glad tidings from great Lucifer.
> Is't not midnight? Come, Mephostophilis,
> *Veni, veni, Mephostophilis!*

> *Enter Mephostophilis.*

> Now tell me what saith Lucifer thy lord?

MEPH.   That I shall wait on Faustus whilst he lives,
        So he will buy my service with his soul.

FAU.   Already Faustus hath **hazarded** that for thee.

Cast consider, ponder.
So on condition that.
hazarded risked.

MEPH.	But now thou must **bequeath** it solemnly	10
	And write a **deed of gift** with thine own blood,	
	For that security craves Lucifer.	
	If thou deny it, I must back to hell.	

FAU. Stay, Mephostophilis, and tell me what good
Will my soul do thy lord?

MEPH.   Enlarge his kingdom.

FAU. Is that the reason why he tempts us thus?

MEPH. **Solamen miseris socios habuisse doloris**.

FAU. Why, have you any pain that torture other?

MEPH. As great as have the human souls of men.
But tell me, Faustus, shall I have thy soul?   20
And I will be thy slave and wait on thee
And give thee more than thou hast wit to ask.

FAU. Ay, Mephostophilis, I'll give it him.

MEPH. Then, Faustus, stab thy arm courageously,
And bind thy soul, that at some certain day
Great Lucifer may claim it as his own;
And then be thou as great as Lucifer.

FAU. Lo, Mephostophilis, for love of thee
Faustus hath cut his arm, and with his **proper** blood
Assures his soul to be great Lucifer's,   30
Chief lord and regent of perpetual night.

---

bequeath hand over, pass on.

deed of gift document or declaration to hand something over.

Solamen . . . **doloris** To unhappy people it is a comfort to have had companions in misfortune.

other others.

wit power of imagination.

binds give a bond for.

proper own.

Assures conveys by deed.

View here this blood that trickles from mine arm,
And let it be **propitious** for my wish.

MEPH. But, Faustus,
Write it in manner of a deed of gift.

FAU. Ay, so I do. But, Mephostophilis,
My blood congeals, and I can write no more.

MEPH. I'll fetch thee fire to dissolve it straight. *(Exit.)*

FAU. What might the **staying** of my blood **portend**?
Is it unwilling I should write this **bill**?   40
Why streams it not, that I may write afresh?
'Faustus gives to thee his soul': O, there it stay'd.
Why shouldst thou not? is not thy soul thine own?
Then write again: 'Faustus gives to thee his soul'.

Enter Mephostophilis with the chafer of fire.

MEPH. See, Faustus, here is fire; set it on.

FAU. So, now the blood begins to clear again:
Now will I make an end immediately.

MEPH. *(aside)* What will not I do to obtain his soul!

FAU. **Consummatum est**: this bill is ended,
And Faustus hath bequeath'd his soul to Lucifer.   50
But what is this inscription on mine arm?
Homo fuge! Whither should I fly?
If unto God, he'll throw me down to hell. –
My senses are deceiv'd, here's nothing writ. –

----

propitious favourable, look kindly on.
staying standing still.
portend give warning of.
bill deed.
chafer portable grate.
Consummatum est It is finished.
Homo fuge! Man, flee!

O yes, I see it plain; even here is writ,
Homo fuge! Yet shall not Faustus fly.

MEPH. *(aside)* I'll fetch him somewhat to delight his mind. *(Exit.)*

*Enter Devils, giving crowns and rich apparel to Faustus. They
dance and then depart. Enter Mephostophilis.*

FAU. What means this **show**? Speak, Mephostophilis.

MEPH. Nothing, Faustus, but to delight thy mind
And let thee see what magic can perform.   60

FAU. But may I raise such spirits when I please?

MEPH. Ay, Faustus, and do greater things than these.

FAU. Then, Mephostophilis, receive this scroll,
A deed of gift of body and of soul:
But yet **conditionally** that thou perform
All **covenants** and **articles** between us both.

MEPH. Faustus, I swear by hell and Lucifer
To effect all promises between us made.

FAU. Then hear me read it, Mephostophilis.

On these conditions following: 70
    *First, that Faustus may be a spirit in form and
substance;*
    *Secondly, that Mephostophilis shall be his servant
and at his command;*
    *Thirdly, that Mephostophilis shall do for him and
bring him whatsoever;*
    *Fourthly, that he shall be in his chamber or house
invisible;*

---

apparel clothes.
show pageant, procession.
conditionally on condition.
covenants agreements, contracts.
articles stipulations, conditions.

Lastly, that he shall appear to the said John Faustus
at all times in what form or shape soever he please;   80
   *I, John Faustus of Wittenberg, doctor, by **these***
***presents** do give both body and soul to Lucifer, prince*
of the east, and his minister Mephostophilis, and
furthermore grant unto them that, four-and-twenty
years being expired, the articles above written
***inviolate**, full power to fetch or carry the said John*
Faustus, body and soul, flesh, blood, or goods, into
their habitation wheresoever.

                              By me John Faustus.

MEPH.   Speak, Faustus, do you deliver this as your deed?

FAU.   Ay, take it, and the devil give thee good **on't**!   90

MEPH.   Now, Faustus, ask what thou wilt.

FAU.   First will I **question with thee** about hell.
         Tell me, where is the place that men call hell?

MEPH.   Under the heavens.

FAU.   Ay, so are all things else; but whereabouts?

MEPH.   Within the bowels of **these elements**,
         Where we are tortur'd and remain for ever.
         Hell hath no limits, nor is **circumscrib'd**
         In **one self place**, but where we are is hell,
         And where hell is, there must we ever be;   100
         And, to be short, when all the world dissolves
         And every creature shall be purify'd,
         All places shall be hell that is not heaven.

---

these presents this present document (a legal term).
inviolate not having been violated or contravened.
on't of it.
question with thee put questions to you.
these elements the elements (earth, water, air, and fire).
circumscrib'd bounded.
one self place one and the same place.

FAU. I think hell's a fable.

MEPH. Ay, think so still, till experience change thy mind.

FAU. Why, dost thou think that Faustus shall be damn'd?

MEPH. Ay, of necessity, for here's the scroll
In which thou hast given thy soul to Lucifer.

C3: Romeo and Juliet

Writer: William Shakespeare

Date: around 1594

Staging: *Romeo and Juliet* was possibly first performed in the Theatre, the first purpose-built playhouse in London, which stood north of the River Thames in Shoreditch. The Theatre was pulled down in 1598 and its timbers taken across the river to Bankside, where it was rebuilt as the Globe a few months later, in 1599. *Romeo and Juliet* was later performed at the Globe.

The story so far

The story takes place in the Italian city of Verona, where two powerful families are constantly in a state of war. Romeo, a Montague, falls in love with Juliet, a Capulet, and, with the help of their friend the Friar, they marry secretly. But, in a street fight, Romeo kills Juliet's cousin and is exiled from the city.

The Friar has a plan to solve their problems. Juliet will take a potion which will make it appear as though she is dead. Her family will place the body in their tomb and Romeo can return in he dead of night to be with her when she awakes from her drugged sleep.

The first part of the plan goes well, and Juliet is laid in the tomb. But Romeo, exiled in Mantua and awaiting news, never receives the letter explaining the Friar's secret plan. This extract comes from the beginning of Act V. Romeo has had a happy dream and is blissfully unaware that his life is about to be destroyed.

ACT V

Scene 1

A street in Mantua. Enter Romeo.

ROMEO   If I may trust the **flattering truth of sleep**,
My dreams **presage** some joyful news at hand.
My bosom's lord sits lightly in his throne;
And all this day an **unaccustomed spirit**
Lifts me above the ground with cheerful thoughts.
I dreamt my lady came and found me dead –
Strange dream that **gives a dead man leave** to think –
And breathed such life with kisses in my lips,
That I revived, and was an emperor.
Ah me, **how sweet is love itself possessed**,   10
When but love's shadows are so rich in joy.

Enter Balthasar his man, booted.

News from Verona. How now Balthasar,
Dost thou not bring me letters from the friar?
How doth my lady? Is my father well?
How doth my Juliet? That I ask again,
For nothing can be ill if she be well.

BALTHASAR   Then she is well and nothing can be ill.
Her body sleeps in Capels' **monument**,

---

flattering truth of sleep Romeo is aware that dreams often tell us what we want to
believe.
presage foretell.
my bosom's lord . . . throne He imagines his heart, which feels light and happy, to be
like a lord, sitting comfortably on his throne.
unaccustomed spirit unusual feeling.
gives . . . leave permits, allows.
how sweet is . . . joy how sweet real, enjoyed love (itself possessed) must be, when
dreams of it can make you so happy!
monument tomb

And her **immortal part** with angels lives.
I saw her laid low in her **kindred**'s vault,   20
And **presently took post** to tell it you.
O pardon me for bringing these ill news,
Since you did leave it for my **office** sir.

ROMEO   **Is it even so?** Then I defy you, stars.
Thou knowest my lodging, get me ink and paper,
And hire **post-horses**; I will hence tonight.

BALTHASAR   I do beseech you sir, have patience.
Your looks are pale and wild, and do **import**
Some misadventure!

ROMEO   **Tush**, thou art deceived.
Leave me, and do the thing I bid you do.   30
Hast thou no letters to me from the friar?

BALTHASAR   No my good lord.

ROMEO   No matter. Get thee gone,
And hire those horses; I'll be with thee straight.

Exit Balthasar.

Well, Juliet, I will **lie with** thee tonight.
Let's see for means. O mischief thou art swift
To enter in the thought of desperate men.
I do remember an **apothecary** –

---

immortal part soul.
kindred family.
presently took post rode here straightaway.
office job, responsibility, duty.
Is it even so? Is that how things are?
post-horses the fastest means of transport.
import some misadventure suggest that some disaster is going to happen.
Tush Nonsense.
lie with 1. = sleep beside; 2. = sexually, as a lover.
Let's see for means How am I going to accomplish this?
apothecary pharmacist, who makes up medicines.

And **hereabouts 'a dwells – which late I noted**,
In tattered weeds, with overwhelming brows
Culling of simples; meagre were his looks,   40
Sharp misery had worn him to the bones;
And in his **needy** shop a tortoise hung,
An alligator stuffed, and other skins
Of ill-shaped fishes, and about his shelves
A **beggarly account** of empty boxes,
Green earthen pots, **bladders**, and musty seeds,
Remnants of packthread, and old **cakes of roses**,
Were thinly scattered, to make up a show.
Noting this **penury**, to myself I said,
'An if a man did need a poison now,   50
Whose sale is present death in Mantua,
Here lives a **caitiff wretch** would sell it him'.
O this same thought did but **forerun my need**,
And this same needy man must sell it me.
As I remember, this should be the house.
Being **holy day**, the beggar's shop is shut.
What ho, apothecary!

---

hereabouts 'a dwells he lives somewhere around here.
which late I noted who I recently spotted.
In tattered weeds . . . in ragged clothes and with overhanging eyebrows.
Culling of simples gathering herbs.
meagre were his looks he was thin-looking.
needy poor.
beggarly account wretchedly small number.
bladders used as containers for liquids.
Remnants of packthread bits of string.
cakes of roses compressed rose petals used as perfume.
penury poverty.
Whose sale is present death . . . the penalty for the sale of this poison in Mantua is immediate death.
caitiff wretch wretched creature ('caitiff' literally means captive).
forerun my need entered my head before I had need of it.
As I remember . . . if I remember rightly . . .
holy day shops were closed on saints' days.

Enter Apothecary.

APOTHECARY   Who calls so loud?

ROMEO   Come hither man. I see that thou art poor.
Hold, there is forty **ducats**, let me have
A dram of poison, such **soon-speeding gear**   60
As will **disperse** itself through all the veins,
That the life-weary taker may fall dead,
And that **the trunk may be discharged of breath**,
As violently as **hasty powder** fired
Doth hurry from the fatal cannon's **womb**.

APOTHECARY   Such **mortal** drugs I have, but Mantua's law
Is death **to any he that utters them**.

ROMEO   **Art thou so bare and full of wretchedness,**
And fearest to die? Famine is in thy cheeks,
Need and oppression starveth in thy eyes   70
Contempt and beggary hangs upon thy back.
The world is not thy friend, nor the world's law,
The world **affords** no law to make thee rich;
Then be not poor, but **break it**, and take this.

---

ducats currency often used in Shakespeare's plays; forty ducats would be a very large sum.

soon-speeding gear fast-acting stuff.

disperse spread.

the trunk . . . breath the body will stop breathing.

hasty powder explosive gun-powder.

womb belly.

mortal deadly, lethal.

to any he . . . them to any man who sells (utters) them.

Art thou . . . die? Can anybody so poor . . . be afraid to die?

Need and . . . eyes I can see your need, oppression and hunger in your eyes.

Contempt and . . . back your clothes show your stage of beggary and the way the world despises you.

affords provides.

break it. 1. = break the law; 2. = break out of your poverty.

APOTHECARY	My poverty, but not my will consents.
ROMEO	I pay thy poverty and not thy will.
APOTHECARY	Put this in any liquid thing you will And drink it off, and if you had the strength Of twenty men, it would **dispatch you straight**.
ROMEO	There is thy gold, worse poison to men's souls, 80 Doing more murder in this loathsome world, Than these poor **compounds** that thou mayst not sell. I sell thee poison, thou hast sold me none. Farewell, buy food, and **get thyself in flesh**. Come **cordial**, and no poison, go with me To Juliet's grave, for there must I use thee.

Exeunt.

Scene 2

Friar Lawrence's cell. Enter Friar John.

| FR JOHN | Holy Franciscan friar, brother, ho! |

Enter Friar Lawrence.

| FR LAWRENCE | This same should be the voice of Friar John.
Welcome from Mantua. What says Romeo?
Or **if his mind be writ**, give me his letter. |
| FR JOHN | Going to find a **bare-foot brother** out, |

---

dispatch you straight kill you instantly.
compounds mixtures.
get thyself in flesh fatten yourself up.
cordial reviving medicine (good for the heart).
if his mind be writ if he has written down his thoughts.
bare-foot brother Franciscan friars travelled barefoot.

One of our **order**, to **associate** me,
Here in this city visiting the sick,
And finding him, the **searchers** of the town,
Suspecting that we both were in a house
Where the infectious **pestilence** did reign,   10
Sealed up the doors, and would not let us **forth**,
So that **my speed to Mantua there was stayed**.

FR LAWRENCE   Who **bare** my letter then to Romeo?

FR JOHN   I could not send it, **here it is again** –
Nor get a messenger to bring it thee,
So fearful were they of infection.

FR LAWRENCE   Unhappy fortune! By my brotherhood,
The letter was not **nice**, but **full of charge**
Of dear import; and the neglecting it
May do much **danger**. Friar John, go hence,   20
Get me an iron **crow** and bring it straight
Unto my cell.

FR JOHN   Brother I'll go and bring it thee. *(Exit.)*

FR LAWRENCE   Now must I to the monument alone;
Within this three hours will fair Juliet wake.
She will **beshrew me much** that Romeo

---

order religious order, community.
associate accompany.
searchers city health inspectors, coroners.
pestilence plague (common in Shakespeare's England).
forth out.
my speed . . . stayed so that I could not get to Mantua.
bare delivered.
here it is again you can have it back.
nice trivial, unimportant.
full of charge . . . import full of serious matters and extremely important.
danger serious harm.
crow crowbar.
beshrew me much curse me severely.

Hath had no notice of these accidents.
But I will write again to Mantua,
And keep her at my cell till Romeo come –
Poor living corse closed in a dead man's tomb.

Exit.

Hath had . . . accidents has received no report about what has happened.

C4: Hamlet

Writer: William Shakespeare
Date: 1601
Staging: The Globe Theatre on Bankside.

The story so far

Hamlet is the Prince of Denmark. When the play begins, his father has just died and his mother has married Claudius, the brother of the dead king, and therefore her brother-in-law. But strange things are happening, and the guards keeping watch on the castle wall have seen a ghost that looks like Hamlet's dead father.

Suspicious about his father's death, and bitter at his mother's hasty remarriage, Hamlet decides to keep watch himself, accompanied by his friend, Horatio. As they stand on the castle battlements in the middle of the freezing night, the ghost appears.

ACT I

Scene 4

Enter Ghost.

HORATIO   Look my lord, it comes.

HAMLET   Angels and ministers of grace defend us.
                    Be thou a spirit of health or goblin damned,
                    Bring with thee airs from heaven, or blasts from hell,
                    Be thy intents wicked, or charitable,
                    Thou com'st in such a questionable shape,
                    That I will speak to thee. I'll call thee Hamlet,
                    King, father, royal Dane. O answer me.
                    Let me not burst in ignorance, but tell
                    Why thy **canonized** bones, hearsed in death,

---

canonized buried in accordance with the rites of the church.

Have burst their **cerements**; why the **sepulchre**,
Wherein we saw thee quietly **interred**,
Hath oped his ponderous and marble jaws,
To cast thee up again. What may this mean,
That thou, dead corse, again in complete steel
Revisits thus the glimpses of the moon,
Making night hideous, and we fools of nature
So horridly to shake our disposition
With thoughts beyond the reaches of our souls?
Say, why is this? Wherefore? What should we do?

Ghost beckons.

HORATIO   It beckons you to go away with it,
As if it some **impartment** did desire
To you alone.

MARCELLUS   Look with what courteous action
It waves you to a more removed ground.
But do not go with it.

HORATIO   No, by no means.

HAMLET   It will not speak; then I will follow it.

HORATIO   Do not my lord.

HAMLET   Why, what should be the fear?
I do not set my life at a **pin's fee**,
And for my soul, what can it do to that
Being a thing immortal as itself?
It waves me forth again. I'll follow it.

HORATIO   What if it tempt you toward the flood my lord,
Or to the dreadful summit of the cliff

cerements burial clothes, waxed cloth to keep a dead body in (modern French *cire*
means wax).
sepulchre tomb.
interred buried.
impartment communication; information.
pin's fee worth a pin.

That **beetles o'er his base** into the sea,
And there assume some other horrible form,
Which might deprive your **sovereignty of reason**
And draw you into madness? Think of it.
The very place puts **toys of desperation**,
Without more motive, into every brain
That looks so many fathoms to the sea,
And hears it roar beneath.

HAMLET   It waves me still.
Go on, I'll follow thee.

MARCELLUS   You shall not go my lord.

HAMLET   Hold off your hands.

HORATIO   Be ruled, you shall not go.

HAMLET   My fate cries out,
And makes each petty artery in this body
As hardy as the **Nemean lion's** nerve.
Still am I called. Unhand me gentlemen.
By heaven I'll make a ghost of him that lets me.
I say, away! Go on, I'll follow thee.

Exeunt Ghost and Hamlet.

HORATIO   He waxes desperate with imagination.

MARCELLUS   Let's follow, 'tis not fit thus to obey him.

HORATIO   Have after. To what issue will this come?

MARCELLUS   Something is rotten in the state of Denmark.

HORATIO   Heaven will direct it.

MARCELLUS   Nay, let's follow him.

Exeunt.

---

beetles o'er his base top of the cliff that hangs over the sea.
sovereignty of reason rule of reason, sense.
toys of desperation desperate fancies.
Nemean lion destroying this lion was one of the labours of Hercules.

Scene 5

Enter Ghost and Hamlet.

HAMLET   Where wilt thou lead me? Speak, I'll go no further.

GHOST   Mark me.

HAMLET   I will.

GHOST   My hour is almost come
When I to sulphurous and tormenting flames
Must render up myself.

HAMLET   Alas poor ghost!

GHOST   Pity me not, but lend thy serious hearing
To what I shall unfold.

HAMLET   Speak, I am bound to hear.

GHOST   So art thou to revenge, when thou shalt hear.

HAMLET   What?

GHOST   I am thy father's spirit,
Doomed for a certain term to walk the night,
And for the day confined to fast in fires,
Till the foul crimes done in my days of nature
Are burnt and purged away. But that I am forbid
To tell the secrets of my prison-house,
I could a tale unfold whose lightest word
Would **harrow up** thy soul, freeze thy young blood,
Make thy two eyes like stars start from their spheres,

Thy knotted and combined locks to part,
And each particular hair to stand an end,
Like quills upon the **fretful porpentine**.
But this **eternal blazon** must not be

---

harrow up tear apart.
fretful porpentine bad-tempered porcupine.
eternal blazon proclamation of what goes on in the immortal world.

	To ears of flesh and blood. **List, list,** o list!
	If thou didst ever thy dear father love –
HAMLET	O God!
GHOST	Revenge his foul and most unnatural murder.
HAMLET	Murder?
GHOST	Murder most foul, as in the best it is,
	But this most foul, strange and unnatural.
HAMLET	Haste me to know 't, that I with wings as swift
	As meditation or the thoughts of love,
	May sweep to my revenge.
GHOST	I find thee apt,
	And duller shouldst thou be than the fat weed
	That roots itself in ease on **Lethe** wharf,
	Wouldst thou not stir in this. Now Hamlet, hear.
	'Tis given out that, sleeping in my orchard,
	A serpent stung me; so the whole ear of Denmark
	Is by a **forged process** of my death
	Rankly abused. But know, thou noble youth,
	The serpent that did sting thy father's life
	Now wears his crown.
HAMLET	O my prophetic soul!
	My uncle?
GHOST	Ay, that incestuous, that adulterate beast,
	With witchcraft of his wits, with traitorous gifts –
	O wicked wit and gifts that have the power
	So to seduce – won to his shameful lust
	The will of my most seeming-virtuous Queen.
	O Hamlet, what a falling-off was there,
	From me whose love was of that dignity

List, list listen.
Lethe the river of forgetfulness in the underworld.
forged process invented description.
Rankly unpleasantly, rudely and coarsely.

That it went hand in hand even with the vow
I made to her in marriage, and to decline
Upon a wretch whose natural gifts were poor
To those of mine.
But virtue, as it never will be moved,
Though lewdness court it **in a shape of heaven**;
So lust, though to a radiant angel linked,
Will **sate** itself in a celestial bed,
And prey on garbage.
But soft, methinks I scent the morning air;
Brief let me be. Sleeping within my orchard,
My custom always of the afternoon,
Upon my **secure hour** thy uncle stole,
With juice of cursed **hebona** in a vial,
And in the porches of my ears did pour
The **leperous distilment**, whose effect
Holds such an enmity with blood of man,
That swift as quicksilver it courses through
The natural gates and alleys of the body,
And with a sudden vigour it doth posset
And curd, like **eager** droppings into milk,
The thin and wholesome blood; so did it mine,
And a most instant **tetter bark'd about**,
Most lazar-like, with vile and loathsome crust
All my smooth body.
Thus was I sleeping, by a brother's hand
Of life, of crown, of queen, at once dispatched;

---

in a shape of heaven disguised as an angel.
sate satisfy.
secure hour period of relaxation.
hebona a poisonous tree or plant – possibly ebony or herbane.
leperous distilment the liquid obtained from a poisonous plant.
eager sour
tetter bark'd about Most lazar-like rough patches suddenly covered my skin, like the
bark of a tree, making me look like a leper.

Cut off even in the blossoms of my sin,
Unhouseled, disappointed, unaneled,
Not reckoning made, but sent to my account
With all my imperfections on my head –
O horrible! O horrible, most horrible!
If thou hast nature in thee, bear it not,
Let not the royal bed of Denmark be
A couch for luxury and damned incest.
But howsoever thou pursuest this act,
Taint not thy mind, nor let thy soul contrive
Against thy mother aught; leave her to heaven,
And to those thorns that in her bosom lodge
To prick and sting her. Fare thee well at once.
The glow-worm shows the **matin** to be near,
And 'gins to pale his uneffectual fire.
Adieu, adieu, adieu. Remember me.

Exit.

HAMLET   O all you host of heaven! O earth! What else?
And shall I couple hell? O fie! Hold, hold, my heart,
And you my sinews, grow not instant old,
But bear me stiffly up. Remember thee?
Ay thou poor ghost, whiles memory holds a seat
In this **distracted globe**. Remember thee?
Yea, from the **table** of my memory
I'll wipe away all trivial fond records,
All saws of books, all forms, all pressures past
That youth and observation copied there,
And thy commandment all alone shall live
Within the book and volume of my brain,

Unhouseled . . . unaneled without the last rites, the sacrament from the priest.
Taint contaminate.
matin morning.
distracted globe his head.
table writing tablet, notebook.

Unmixed with baser matter – yes, by heaven!
O most **pernicious** woman!
O villain, villain, smiling, damned villain!
My tables – meet it is I set it down,
That one may smile, and smile, and be a villain;
At least I am sure it may be so in Denmark:

Writes.

So uncle, there you are. Now to my word;
It is 'Adieu, adieu, remember me'.
I have sworn't.

---

pernicious wicked, harmful.

Activities: Section C, Tragedy.

C1: The Agamemnon, page 110.

1   In groups of five or six, make up a series of freeze-frames which
    help to illustrate the story. Start with the moment at the beginning
    of the extract at which Agamemnon is faced with his terrible
    dilemma.

    - When you have decided on the freeze-frames, act out each one
      while other people read out the Chorus lines.
    - Finally, discuss a) exactly what choices were facing
      Agamemnon; and b) what you think he should have done.

2   The stories of the great siege of Troy and what happened
    afterwards were retold in poems and plays by many writers,
    including the ancient Greek poet, Homer (in *The Iliad* and *The
    Odyssey* from the eighth century BCE), and the Roman poet, Virgil
    (in the Latin *Æneid* from the first century CE). Many writers still
    draw upon these stories for inspiration. In your groups, check that
    you know the main details of the following episodes, all to do with
    the siege of Troy and its aftermath:

    - Achilles being shot by an arrow
    - Odysseus (known to the Romans as Ulysses) devising a plan
      which involved a wooden horse.

3   Imagine you are making a film of *The Agamemnon*. Draw a series
    of storyboards for a sequence based on this extract.

    - Underneath each frame, write the lines of the Chorus which can
      be heard in 'voice-over'.
    - Finally, write a short commentary to explain why you have
      chosen these particular shots.

C2: Doctor Faustus, page 114.

1   Read the scene in pairs. Now imagine you are staging it and make
    some notes on the visual aspects of the scene – what the audience
    will see.

    • For example, what should Mephostophilis look like? Think about
      his costume and make-up.
    • Should there be any special effects when he appears?
    • How will you show Faustus writing in blood from his arm?
    • What should the devils look like, conjured by up Mephostophilis
      to distract Faustus?
    • What do they do when they appear?

2   Re-read the agreement that Faustus has signed (lines 70–88).

    • What powers does Faustus now have and why does he want
      them?
    • What does Faustus hope to be able to do?
    • What is the first question that Faustus asks after he has signed?
      What does that tell us about him?

3   Write an account of the scene from Mephostophilis's viewpoint, in
    which he explains why he wanted Faustus's soul and exactly what
    happened.

    • What does Mephostophilis say about the agreement?
    • What does he predict will happen in the next twenty-four years?

C3: Romeo and Juliet, page 120.

1   In many plays, from the time of the ancient Greeks onwards, Fate
    is presented as a force which dictates that certain things will
    happen and there is nothing we can do about it. In this play, Fate
    seems to have taken a hand when Romeo, at his happiest after
    marrying Juliet, gets involved in a fight which leads to his exile for
    killing Juliet's cousin. In pairs, re-read the scenes, and discuss the

part played by Fate in causing Romeo to take the action he does.

2   We perhaps fear the worst at the opening of Scene 1, when Romeo tells us that he has had a dream in which 'my lady came and found me dead' (line 6).

- Re-read the extract and note down all the references to death which follow this speech.
- Pick one image and draw a sketch of the picture that comes into your mind.
- Then write a sentence or two to explain how your drawing reflects what is in the text.

3   Two different film versions (the 1968 film directed by Franco Zeffirelli and the 1997 film directed by Baz Luhrmann) dealt with Friar John's account of the undelivered letter in Scene 2 by cutting him out of the story altogether and simply showing a version of the events he describes.

a)   The 1968 film simply showed Friar John leaving the city, carrying the letter from Friar Lawrence to Romeo, travelling on the back of a donkey. As he trots along a dusty lane, Balthasar gallops past him on horseback – he will plainly get to Romeo first.

b)   The 1997 film, set in modern-day America, showed a mail-man trying in vain to deliver the letter at the front door of the mobile-home, or camper, in which Romeo is staying. He doesn't notice that Romeo is sitting out the back, so he leaves an official note informing Romeo to collect mail. Balthasar arrives and delivers his news, and we see the mail-man's note being blown away.

In pairs, decide which of the three versions (Shakespeare's script and the two films) is most effective in showing how cruel Fate can be and how we have no influence over it.

- Then write an outline of a film sequence of your own which shows the power of Fate over our lives.

C4: Hamlet, page 128.

1   This extract is taken from the first Act of the play. Later on, Hamlet
    arranges for a company of actors to perform a play in front of
    Claudius which has a plot very similar to the story of his father's
    murder. They begin with a 'dumb-show', or mime, which outlines
    the story for the audience, but without words. In groups of three,
    create the mime which might introduce their play.

2   In your groups, make a list of other stories (films, plays, novels,
    etc) which involve revenge of some kind. Think about what
    happens in these revenge stories and make a list of the typical
    features of the revenge genre. For example, revenge stories have
    to start with a wicked deed of some kind.

3   We find later in the play that Hamlet always keeps a notebook with
    him (his 'tables'), so that he can jot down interesting things that
    he has heard. Imagine you are Hamlet. What would you write in
    your notebook about your encounter with the ghost? What did you
    see? How does it make you feel? What do you think you will do
    now?

Section D: Viewpoints on Society

Many playwrights, from the ancient Greeks onwards, have used plays to get their ideas across and to make audiences aware of things that are going on. The extracts in this section represent the different ways in which a play might be called 'social' or 'political' drama. It might, for example:

- have a general moral message it wants to get across, such as the fact that we are all responsible for one another (as in *An Inspector Calls*);
- want to expose a society's values and show that things are going badly wrong (*Loot*);
- focus on a general topic, such as the position of women in society (*Top Girls*);
- represent the changes a society is undergoing (*I Will Marry When I Want*);
- expose the ills of a particular political system, such as apartheid in South Africa (*Sizwe Bansi is Dead*);
- attack people's greed (*Volpone*).

Some of these plays about society contain **satire**: a kind of comedy which exposes people's faults or vices with the aim of making them behave better. Satire is used to make audiences laugh at just how insane, dishonest and hypocritical human beings can be.

D1: An Inspector Calls

Writer: J.B. Priestley
Date: 1947
Staging: A realistic set, to represent a dining-room in the house of a well-off northern family at the beginning of the twentieth century.

The story so far

Five people have just finished a very good meal. They are the wealthy factory owner, Birling, his wife, their son Eric, their daughter Sheila, and her fiancé Gerald. As was the custom in those days, the women have left the room and the two younger men are listening to Birling, when there is a ring on the front door.

Birling has just been advising the younger men that it is every man for himself in this world, when the maid introduces the visitor as Inspector Goole. The Inspector reports that a young woman, Eva Smith, has just committed suicide in the local hospital. Birling admits to having known her – she once worked in his factory – but denies having anything to do with her suicide. The Inspector, however, suggests that her time in Birling's factory might well have a connection with her death.

INSPECTOR	Because what happened to her then may have determined what happened to her afterwards, and what happened to her afterwards may have driven her to suicide. A chain of events.
BIRLING	Oh well – put like that, there's something in what you say. Still, I can't accept any responsibility. If we were all responsible for everything that happened to everybody we'd had anything to do with, it would be very awkward, wouldn't it?
INSPECTOR	Very awkward.
BIRLING	We'd all be in an impossible position, wouldn't we?

ERIC	By Jove, yes. And as you were saying, Dad, a man has to look after himself –
BIRLING	Yes, well, we needn't go into all that.
INSPECTOR	Go into what?
BIRLING	Oh – just before you came – I'd been giving these young men a little good advice. Now – about this girl, Eva Smith. I remember her quite well now. She was a lively good-looking girl – country bred, I fancy – and she'd been working in one of our machine shops for over a year. A good worker too. In fact, the foreman there told me he was ready to promote her into what we call a leading operator – head of a small group of girls. But after they came back from their holidays that August, they were all rather restless, and they suddenly decided to ask for more money. They were averaging about twenty-two and six, which was neither more nor less than is paid generally in our industry. They wanted the rates so that they could average about twenty-five shillings a week. I refused, of course.
INSPECTOR	Why?
BIRLING	*(surprised)* Did you say 'Why?'?
INSPECTOR	Yes. Why did you refuse?
BIRLING	Well, Inspector, I don't see that it's any concern of yours how I choose to run my business. Is it now?
INSPECTOR	It might be, you know.
BIRLING	I don't like that tone.
INSPECTOR	I'm sorry. But you asked me a question.
BIRLING	And you asked me a question before that, a quite unnecessary question too.
INSPECTOR	It's my duty to ask questions.

BIRLING	Well, it's my duty to keep labour costs down, and if I'd agreed to this demand for a new rate we'd have added about twelve per cent to our labour costs. Does that satisfy you? So I refused. Said I couldn't consider it. We were paying the usual rates and if they didn't like those rates, they could go and work somewhere else. It's a free country, I told them.
ERIC	It isn't if you can't go and work somewhere else.
INSPECTOR	Quite so.
BIRLING	*(to Eric)* Look – just you keep out of this. You hadn't even started in the works when this happened. So they went on strike. That didn't last long, of course.
GERALD	Not if it was just after the holidays. They'd be all broke – if I know them.
BIRLING	Right, Gerald. They mostly were. And so was the strike, after a week or two. Pitiful affair. Well, we let them all come back – at the old rates – except the four or five ring-leaders, who'd started the trouble. I went down myself and told them to clear out. And this girl, Eva Smith, was one of them. She'd had a lot to say – far too much – so she had to go.
GERALD	You couldn't have done anything else.
ERIC	He could. He could have kept her on instead of throwing her out. I call it tough luck.
BIRLING	Rubbish! If you don't come down sharply on some of these people, they'd soon be asking for the earth.
GERALD	I should say so!
INSPECTOR	They might. But after all it's better to ask for the earth than to take it.

[. . .]

SHEILA	I've told my father – he didn't seem to think it amounted to much – but I felt rotten about it at the time and now I feel a lot worse. Did it make much difference to her?
INSPECTOR	Yes, I'm afraid it did. It was the last real steady job she had. When she lost it – for no reason that she could discover – she decided she might as well try another kind of life.
SHEILA	*(miserably)* So I'm really responsible?
INSPECTOR	No, not entirely. A good deal happened to her after that. But you're partly to blame. Just as your father is.
ERIC	But what did Sheila do?
SHEILA	*(distressed)* I went to the manager at Milwards and I told him that if they didn't get rid of that girl, I'd never go near the place again and I'd persuade mother to close our account with them.
INSPECTOR	And why did you do that?
SHEILA	Because I was in a furious temper.
INSPECTOR	And what had this girl done to make you lose your temper?
SHEILA	When I was looking at myself in the mirror I caught sight of her smiling at the assistant, and I was furious with her. I'd been in a bad temper anyhow.
INSPECTOR	And was it the girl's fault?
SHEILA	No, not really. It was my own fault. *(Suddenly, to Gerald)* All right, Gerald, you needn't look at me like that. At least, I'm trying to tell the truth. I expect you've done things you're ashamed of too.
GERALD	*(surprised)* Well, I never said I hadn't. I don't see why –

INSPECTOR	*(cutting in)* Never mind about that. You can settle that between you afterwards. *(To Sheila)* What happened?
SHEILA	I'd gone in to try something on. It was an idea of my own – mother had been against it, and so had the assistant – but I insisted. As soon as I tried it on, I knew they'd been right. It just didn't suit me at all. I looked silly in the thing. Well, this girl had brought the dress up from the workroom, and when the assistant – Miss Francis – had asked her something about it, this girl, to show us what she meant, had held the dress up, as if she was wearing it. And it just suited her. She was the right type for it, just as I was the wrong type. She was a very pretty girl too – with big dark eyes – and that didn't make it any better. Well, when I tried the thing on and looked at myself and knew that it was all wrong, I caught sight of this girl smiling at Miss Francis – as if to say: 'Doesn't she look awful' – and I was absolutely furious. I was very rude to both of them, and then I went to the manager and told him that this girl had been very impertinent – and – and *(She almost breaks down but just controls herself.)* How could I know what would happen afterwards? If she'd been some miserable plain little creature, I don't suppose I'd have done it. But she was very pretty and looked as if she could take care of herself. I couldn't be sorry for her.
INSPECTOR	In fact, in a kind of way, you might be said to have been jealous of her.
SHEILA	Yes, I suppose so.
INSPECTOR	And so you used the power you had, as a daughter of a good customer and also of a man well known in the town, to punish the girl just because she made you feel like that?

SHEILA Yes, but it didn't seem to be anything very terrible at the time. Don't you understand? And if I could help her now, I would –

INSPECTOR *(harshly)* Yes, but you can't. It's too late. She's dead.

D2: I Will Marry When I Want

Writers: Ngugi wa Thiong'o and Ngugi wa Mirii
Date: 1982
Staging: The play takes place in the home of Kiguunda, a farm labourer, and his wife and daughter, Wangeci and Gathoni. The opening stage directions read:

Kiguunda's home. A square, mud-walled, white-ochred, one-roomed house. The white ochre is fading. In one corner can be seen Kiguunda and Wangeci's bed. In another can be seen a pile of rags on the floor. The floor is Gathoni's bed and the rags, her bedding. Although poorly dressed, Gathoni is very beautiful. In the same room can be seen a pot on three stones. On one of the walls there hangs a framed title-deed for one and a half acres of land. Near the head of the bed, on the wall, there hangs a sheathed sword. On one side of the wall there hangs Kiguunda's coat, and on the opposite side, on the same wall, Wangeci's coat. The coats are torn and patched. A pair of tyre sandals and a basin can be seen on the floor.

The story so far
When this scene opens, a short way into the play, Kiguunda has just heard that they are to receive a visit from the wealthy farm owner and his wife, Kioi and Jezebel.

WANGECI	I wonder what Mr Kioi And Jezebel, his madam, Want in a poor man's home? Why did they take all that trouble to let us know beforehand That they would be coming here today?
KIGUUNDA	You, you woman, Even if you see me in these tatters I am not poor.

He shows her the title-deed by pointing at it. Then he hangs it back on the wall.

You should know
That a man without debts is not poor at all.
Aren't we the ones who make them rich?
Were it not for my blood and sweat
And the blood and sweat of all the other workers,
Where would the likes of Kioi and his wife now be?
Tell me!
Where would they be today?

WANGECI Leave me alone,
You'll keep on singing the same song
Till the day you people wake up.
A fool's walking stick supports the clever.
But why do you sit idle
While this bedframe
Also needs a nail or two?

Kiguunda takes the hammer and goes to repair the bed. Wangeci turns her face and sees Gathoni's bedding on the floor.

Gathoni, Gathoni!

GATHONI Yes!

WANGECI Gathoni!

GATHONI Yeees!

WANGECI Can't you help me
In peeling potatoes,
In sorting out the rice,
Or in looking after the fire?
Instead of sitting there,
Legs stretched,
Plaiting your hair?

GATHONI Mother you love complaining

Haven't I just swept the floor?

WANGECI And what is that bedding doing over there?
Can't you put it somewhere in a corner,
Or else take it outside to the sun
So the fleas can fly away?

GATHONI These tatters!
Are these what you call bedding?
And this floor,
Is this what you call a bed?

WANGECI Why don't you get yourself a husband
Who'll buy you spring beds?

GATHONI Mother, why are you insulting me?
Is that why you refused to send me to school,
So that I may remain your slave,
And for ever toil for you?
Picking tea and coffee only for you to pocket the wages?
And all that so that you can get money
To pay fees for your son!
Do you want me to remain buried under these ashes?
And on top of all that injury
You have to abuse me night and day?
Do you think I cannot get a husband?
I'll be happy the day I leave this home!

WANGECI *(with sarcasm)* Take to the road!
There's no girl worth the name
Who is contented with being an old maid
In her mother's homestead.

GATHONI Sorry!
I shall marry when I want.
Nobody will force me into it!

WANGECI What? What did you say?

GATHONI I shall marry when I want.

WANGECI You dare talk back to me like that?

Oh, my clansmen, come!
You have started to insult me at your age?
Why don't you wait until you have grown some teeth!
(With sarcasm) You! Let me warn you.
If I was not expecting some guests
I would teach you never to abuse your mother.
Take these potato peelings and throw them out in
    the yard.

*Gathoni takes the peelings. As she is about to go out, her
father shouts at her.*

KIGUUNDA   Gathoni!

Gathoni looks at her father fearfully.

Come here.

Gathoni makes only one step forward still in fear.

If ever I see or hear that again . . . !
Utaona cha mtema kuni.
Do you think that we mine gold,
To enable us to educate boys and girls?
Go away!
Na uchunge mdomo wako.

Gathoni takes the peelings out.

WANGECI   What's wrong with the child?
She used not to be like this!

KIGUUNDA   It's all the modern children.
They have no manners at all.
In my time
We could not even sneeze in front of our parents.
What they need is a whip
To make them straighten up!

WANGECI   No!

When children get to that age,
We can only watch them and hope for the best.
When axes are kept in one basket they must
    necessarily knock against each other.
She'll soon marry and be out of sight.
There's no maiden who makes a home in her father's
    backyard.
And there's no maiden worth the name who wants to
    get grey hairs at her parents' home.

D3: Sizwe Bansi is Dead

Writers: Athol Fugard, John Kani, Winston Ntshona
Date: 1972
Staging: This was written to be performed in classrooms, village halls, bars – anywhere. The set, therefore, is made up of simple pieces of furniture and props which can be easily and quickly removed.

The story so far

The events take place at the height of apartheid in South Africa – the political system which classed the black population as inferior, and under which they suffered great loss of freedom. All black people at this time had to carry a passbook, which was stamped regularly to show the area of the country in which they were allowed to work – often a very long way from their home and family. If your passbook stated that you were only allowed to work in one city, you could not get a job in another.

In this play, Sizwe (called MAN in the script) has had his passbook stamped to say that he has to leave Port Elizabeth in three days' time. Desperate for a job, he decides to hide in a friend's house, but one night the building is raided. Sizwe is taken to the police station and ordered to report to King William's Town, a long way off.

Later that night, he is walking through a tough part of town, talking over his problem with a friend called Buntu, when they discover a body down an alley. Looking at the dead man's passbook, they discover that he is Robert Zwelinzima, and that he has a stamp which allows him to look for work. This gives Buntu an idea . . .

A thoughtful Buntu rejoins him, the dead man's reference book still in his hand.

BUNTU   Let me see your book?

Sizwe doesn't respond.

Give me your book!

*MAN   Are you a policeman now, Buntu?

BUNTU   Give me your bloody book, Sizwe!

MAN   *(handing it over)* Take it, Buntu. Take this book and read it carefully, friend, and tell me what it says about me. Buntu, does that book tell you I'm a man?

Buntu studies the two books. Sizwe turns back to the audience.

That bloody book . . . ! People, do you know? No! Wherever you go . . . it's that bloody book. You go to school, it goes too. Go to work, it goes too. Go to church and pray and sing lovely hymns, it sits there with you. Go to hospital to die, it lies there too!

Buntu has collected Sizwe's discarded clothing.

BUNTU   Come!

Buntu's house, as earlier. Table and two chairs. Buntu pushes Sizwe down into a chair. Sizwe still muttering, starts to struggle back into his clothes. Buntu opens the two reference books and places them side by side on the table. He produces a pot of glue, then very carefully tears out the photograph in each book. A dab of glue on the back of each and then Sizwe's goes back into Robert's book, and Robert's into Sizwe's. Sizwe watches this operation, at first uninterestedly, but when he realises what Buntu is up to, with growing alarm. When he is finished, Buntu pushes the two books in front of Sizwe.

MAN   *(shaking his head emphatically)* Yo! *Haai, haai.* No, Buntu.

BUNTU   It's a chance.

MAN   **Haai,** *haai, haai . . .*

---

*Sizwe is called MAN as he has more than one name.
Haai an exclamation of surprise.

BUNTU	It's your only chance!
MAN	No, Buntu! What's it mean? That me, Sizwe Bansi . . .
BUNTU	Is dead.
MAN	I'm not dead, friend.
BUNTU	We burn this book . . . *(Sizwe's original)* . . . and Sizwe Bansi disappears off the face of the earth.
MAN	What about the man we left lying in the alleyway?
BUNTU	Tomorrow the Flying Squad passes there and finds him. Check in his pockets . . . no passbook. Mount Road Mortuary. After three days nobody has identified him. Pauper's Burial. Case closed.
MAN	And then?
BUNTU	Tomorrow I contact my friend Norman at Feltex. He's a boss-boy there. I tell him about another friend, Robert Zwelinzima, book in order, who's looking for a job. You roll up later, hand over the book to the white man. Who does Robert Zwelinzima look like? You! Who gets the pay on Friday? You, man!
MAN	What about all that shit at the Labour Bureau, Buntu?
BUNTU	You don't have to there. This chap had a work-seekers permit, Sizwe. All you do is hand over the book to the white man. *He* checks at the Labour Bureau. They check with their big machine. 'Robert Zwelinzima has the right to be employed and stay in this town.'
MAN	I don't want to lose my name, Buntu.
BUNTU	You mean you don't want to lose your bloody passbook! You love it, hey?
MAN	Buntu. I cannot lose my name.
BUNTU	*(leaving the table)* All right, I was only trying to help. As Robert Zwelinzima you could have stayed and worked in this town. As Sizwe Bansi . . . ? Start walking, friend. King

William's Town. Hundred and fifty miles. And don't waste any time! You've got to be there by yesterday. Hope you enjoy it.

MAN   Buntu . . .

BUNTU Lots of scenery in a hundred and fifty miles.

MAN   Buntu! . . .

BUNTU Maybe a better idea is just to wait until they pick you up. Save yourself all that walking. Into the train with the escort! Smart stuff, hey. Hope it's not too crowded though. Hell of a lot of people being kicked out, I hear.

MAN   Buntu! . . .

BUNTU But once you're back! Sit down on the side of the road next to your **pondok** with your family . . . the whole Bansi clan on leave . . . for life! Hey, that sounds okay. Watching all the cars passing, and as you say, friend, cough your bloody lungs out with **Ciskeian Independence**.

MAN   *(now really desperate)* Buntu!!!

BUNTU What you waiting for? Go!

MAN   Buntu.

BUNTU What?

MAN   What about my wife, Nowetu?

BUNTU What about her?

MAN   *(maudlin tears)* Her loving husband, Sizwe Bansi, is dead!

BUNTU So what! She's going to marry a better man.

MAN   *(bridling)* Who?

BUNTU You . . . Robert Zwelinzima

---

pondok shack, shanty.
Ciskeian Independence Ciskei was one of the black homelands created by the South African government. Buntu regards it as a dusty waste land.

MAN	*(thoroughly confused)* How can I marry my wife, Buntu?
BUNTU	Get her down here and I'll introduce you.
MAN	Don't make jokes, Buntu. Robert . . . Sizwe . . . I'm all mixed up. Who am I?
BUNTU	A fool who is not taking his chance.
MAN	And my children! Their father is Sizwe Bansi. They're registered at school under Bansi . . .
BUNTU	Are you really worried about your children, friend, or are you just worried about yourself and your bloody name? Wake up, man! Use that book and with your pay on Friday you'll have a real chance to do something for them.
MAN	I'm afraid. How do I get used to Robert? How do I live as another man's ghost?
BUNTU	Wasn't Sizwe Bansi a ghost?
MAN	No!
BUNTU	No? When the white man looked at you at the Labour Bureau what did he see? A man with dignity or a bloody passbook with an N.I. number? Isn't that a ghost? When the white man sees you walk down the street and calls out, 'Hey, John! Come here' . . . to you, *Sizwe Bansi* . . . isn't that a ghost? Or when his little child calls you 'Boy' . . . you a man, circumcised with a wife and four children . . . isn't that a ghost? Stop fooling yourself. All I'm saying is be a real ghost, if that is what they want, what they've turned us into. Spook them into hell, man!

Sizwe is silenced. Buntu realises his words are beginning to reach the other man. He paces quietly, looking for his next move. He finds it.

Suppose you try my plan. Friday. Roughcasting section at Feltex. Paytime. Line of men – non-skilled labourers.

White man with the big box full of pay-packets.
'**John Kani!**' 'Yes, sir!' Pay-packet is handed over. 'Thank you, sir.'
Another one. *(Buntu reads the name on an imaginary pay-packet.)* '**Winston Ntshona!**' Yes, sir!' Pay-packet over. 'Thank you, sir!' Another one. '**Fats Bhokolane!**' *'Hier is ek, my baas!'* Pay-packet over. '**Dankie, my baas!**' Another one. 'Robert Zwelinzima!'

No response from Sizwe.

'Robert Zwelinzima!'

MAN   Yes, sir.

BUNTU   *(handing him the imaginary pay-packet)* Open it. Go on.

Takes back the packet, tears it open, empties its contents on the table, and counts it.

Five . . . ten . . . eleven . . . twelve . . . and ninety-nine cents. In *your* pocket!

Buntu again paces quietly, leaving Sizwe to think. Eventually . . .

Saturday. Man in overalls, twelve rand ninety-nine cents in the back pocket, walking down Main Street looking for Sales House. Finds it and walks in. Salesman comes forward to meet him.
'I've come to buy a suit.' Salesman is very friendly.
'Certainly. Won't you take a seat. I'll get the forms. I'm sure you want to open an account, sir. Six months to pay. But first I'll need all your particulars.'

John Kani . . . **Winston Ntshona** . . . **Fats Bhokolane** an in-joke as these are the names of actors who have performed the play.
Hier is ek, my baas Here I am, boss! (in Afrikaans, the language of the Dutch settlers).
Dankie, my baas Thank you, boss!

Buntu has turned the table, with Sizwe on the other side, into the imaginary scene at Sales House.

BUNTU *(pencil poised, ready to fill in a form)* Your name, please, sir?

MAN *(playing along uncertainly)* Robert Zwelinzima.

BUNTU *(writing)* 'Robert Zwelinzima.' Address?

MAN Fifty, Mapija Street.

BUNTU Where do you work?

MAN Feltex.

BUNTU And how much do you get paid?

MAN Twelve . . . twelve rand ninety-nine cents.

BUNTU N.I. Number, please?

Sizwe hesitates.

Your Native Identity number please?

Sizwe is still uncertain. Buntu abandons the act and picks up Robert Zwelinzima's passbook. He reads out the number.

N–I–3–8–1–1–8–6–3.
Burn that into your head, friend. You hear me? It's more important than your name.
N.I. number . . . three . . .

MAN Three.

BUNTU Eight.

MAN Eight.

BUNTU One.

MAN One.

BUNTU One.

MAN One.

BUNTU Eight.

MAN Eight.

BUNTU	Six.
MAN	Six.
BUNTU	Three.
MAN	Three.
BUNTU	Again. Three.
MAN	Three.
BUNTU	Eight.
MAN	Eight.
BUNTU	One.
MAN	One.
BUNTU	One.
MAN	One.
BUNTU	Eight.
MAN	Eight.
BUNTU	Six.
MAN	Six.
BUNTU	Three.
MAN	Three.
BUNTU	*(picking up his pencil and returning to the role of the salesman)* N.I. number, please.
MAN	*(pausing frequently, using his hands to remember)* Three . . . eight . . . one . . . one . . . eight . . . six . . . three . . .
BUNTU	*(abandoning the act)* Good boy.

D4: Top Girls

Writer: Caryl Churchill
Date: 1982
Staging: A neutral background, with realistic furniture and props added for each scene, to represent a restaurant, an employment agency, a backyard and a kitchen.

The story so far

This scene takes place quite near the beginning of the play. Marlene, a businesswoman, has booked a table in a restaurant. When the other diners arrive, we see that they are characters from history, legend, art and literature: the traveller Isabella Bird (who died in 1904); Lady Nijo, a thirteenth-century Japanese courtesan, or prostitute, who later became a Buddhist nun; Dull Gret, a fierce character out of a painting by the sixteenth-century artist, Breughel; Pope Joan, who, disguised as a man, is believed to have been Pope between 854 and 856; and Patient Griselda, the obedient wife whose story is told by Chaucer in one of the fourteenth-century *Canterbury Tales*. In this sequence, Griselda tells her story.

Points to note

One very unusual feature of the writing is that the characters' speeches overlap each other, as they do in real conversations. To read this dialogue out loud, you need to know that:

- when one character starts speaking before the other has finished, the point where they interrupt is marked /
- sometimes a character carries on speaking right through another character's speech
- sometimes a speech follows on from a speech earlier than the one immediately before it. The end of the earlier speech and the continuation of it are marked *

ACT ONE

Scene 1

Marlene notices Griselda . . .

MARLENE	Griselda! / There you are. Do you want to eat?
GRISELDA	I'm sorry I'm so late. No, no, don't bother.
MARLENE	Of course it's no bother. / Have you eaten?
GRISELDA	No really, I'm not hungry.
MARLENE	Well, have some pudding.
GRISELDA	I never eat pudding.
MARLENE	Griselda, I hope you're not anorexic. We're having pudding, I am, and getting nice and fat.
GRISELDA	Oh if everyone is. I don't mind.
MARLENE	Now who do you know? This is Joan who was Pope in the ninth century, and Isabella Bird, the Victorian traveller, and Lady Nijo from Japan, Emperor's concubine and Buddhist nun, thirteenth century, nearer your own time, and Gret who was painted by Brueghel. Griselda's in Boccaccio and Petrarch and Chaucer because of her extraordinary marriage. I'd like profiteroles because they're disgusting.
JOAN	Zabaglione, please.
ISABELLA	Apple pie / and cream.
NIJO	What's this?
MARLENE	Zabaglione, it's Italian, it's what Joan's having, / it's delicious.
NIJO	A Roman Catholic / dessert? Yes please.
MARLENE	Gret?
GRET	Cake.
GRISELDA	Just cheese and biscuits, thank you.

Line numbers in the right margin: 10 (at "Now who do you know?"), 20 (at "What's this?").

MARLENE	Yes, Griselda's life is like a fairy-story, except it starts with marrying the prince.
GRISELDA	He's only a marquis, Marlene.
MARLENE	Well, everyone for miles around is his liege and he's 30 absolute lord of life and death and you were the poor but beautiful peasant girl and he whisked you off. / Near enough a prince.
NIJO	How old were you?
GRISELDA	Fifteen.
NIJO	I was brought up in court circles and it was still a shock. Had you ever seen him before?
GRISELDA	I'd seen him riding by, we all had. And he'd seen me in the fields with the sheep. *
ISABELLA	I would have been well suited to minding sheep. 40
NIJO	And Mr Nugent riding by.
ISABELLA	Of course not, Nijo, I mean a healthy life in the open air.
JOAN	* He just rode up while you were minding the sheep and asked you to marry him?
GRISELDA	No, no, it was on the wedding day. I was waiting outside the door to see the procession. Everyone wanted him to get married so there'd be an heir to look after us when he died, / and at last he announced a day for the wedding but 50
MARLENE	I don't think Walter wanted to get married. It is Walter? Yes.
GRISELDA	nobody knew who the bride was, we thought it must be a foreign princess, we were longing to see her. Then the carriage stopped outside our cottage and we couldn't see the bride anywhere. And he came and spoke to my father.

NIJO	And your father told you to serve the Prince.
GRISELDA	My father could hardly speak. The Marquis said it wasn't an order, I could say no, but if I said yes I must always obey him in everything. 60
MARLENE	That's when you should have suspected.
GRISELDA	But of course a wife must obey her husband. / And of course I must obey the Marquis. *
ISABELLA	I swore to obey dear John, of course, but it didn't seem to arise. Naturally I wouldn't have wanted to go abroad while I was married.
MARLENE	* Then why bother to mention it at all? He'd got a thing about it, that's why.
GRISELDA	I'd rather obey the Marquis than a boy from the village. 70
MARLENE	Yes, that's a point.
JOAN	I never obeyed anyone. They all obeyed me.
NIJO	And what did you wear? He didn't make you get married in your own clothes? That would be perverse. *
MARLENE	Oh, you wait.
GRISELDA	* He had ladies with him who undressed me and they had a white silk dress and jewels for my hair.
MARLENE	And at first he seemed perfectly normal?
GRISELDA	Marlene, you're always so critical of him. / Of course he was normal, he was very kind. 80
MARLENE	But Griselda, come on, he took your baby.
GRISELDA	Walter found it hard to believe I loved him. He couldn't believe I would always obey him. He had to prove it.
MARLENE	I don't think Walter likes women.
GRISELDA	I'm sure he loved me, Marlene, all the time.
MARLENE	He just had a funny way / of showing it.

GRISELDA	It was hard for him too.
JOAN	How do you mean he took away your baby? 90
NIJO	Was it a boy?
GRISELDA	No, the first one was a girl.
NIJO	Even so it's hard when they take it away. Did you see it at all?
GRISELDA	Oh yes, she was six weeks old.
NIJO	Much better to do it straight away.
ISABELLA	But why did your husband take the child?
GRISELDA	He said all the people hated me because I was just one of them. And now I had a child they were restless. So he had to get rid of the child to keep them quiet. 100 But he said he wouldn't snatch her, I had to agree and obey and give her up. So when I was feeding her a man came in and took her away. I thought he was going to kill her even before he was out of the room.
MARLENE	But you let him take her? You didn't struggle?
GRISELDA	I asked him to give her back so I could kiss her. And I asked him to bury her where no animals could dig her up. / It
ISABELLA	Oh my dear.
GRISELDA	was Walter's child to do what he liked with. * 110
MARLENE	Walter was bonkers.
GRET	Bastard.
ISABELLA	* But surely, murder.
GRISELDA	I had promised.
MARLENE	I can't stand this. I'm going for a pee.

Marlene goes out. The Waitress brings dessert.

NIJO	No, I understand. Of course you had to, he was your life. And were you in favour after that?

GRISELDA	Oh yes, we were very happy together. We never spoke about what had happened.
ISABELLA	I can see you were doing what you thought was your duty. But didn't it make you ill?
GRISELDA	No, I was very well, thank you.
NIJO	And you had another child?
GRISELDA	Not for four years, but then I did, yes, a boy.
NIJO	Ah a boy. / So it all ended happily.
GRISELDA	Yes, he was pleased. I kept my son till he was two years old. A peasant's grandson. It made the people angry. Walter explained.
ISABELLA	But surely he wouldn't kill his children / just because –
GRISELDA	Oh it wasn't true. Walter would never give in to the people. He wanted to see if I loved him enough.
JOAN	He killed his children / to see if you loved him enough?
NIJO	Was it easier the second time or harder?
GRISELDA	It was always easy because I always knew I would do what he said.

Pause. They start to eat.

ISABELLA	I hope you didn't have any more children.
GRISELDA	Oh no, no more. It was twelve years till he tested me again.
ISABELLA	So whatever did he do this time? / My poor John, I never loved him enough, and he would never have dreamt . . .
GRISELDA	He sent me away. He said the people wanted him to marry someone else who'd give him an heir and he'd got special permission from the Pope. So I said I'd go home to my father. I came with nothing / so I went with nothing. I

NIJO	Better to leave if your master doesn't want you.
GRISELDA	took off my clothes. He let me keep a slip so he wouldn't be shamed. And I walked home barefoot. My father came out in tears. Everyone was crying except me.

150

NIJO	At least your father wasn't dead. / I had nobody.
ISABELLA	Well, it can be a relief to come home. I loved to see Hennie's sweet face again.
GRISELDA	Oh yes, I was perfectly content. And quite soon he sent for me again.
JOAN	I don't think I would have gone.
GRISELDA	But he told me to come. I had to obey him. He wanted me to help prepare his wedding. He was getting married to a young girl from France / and nobody except me knew how to arrange things the way he liked them.

160

NIJO	It's always hard taking him another woman.

Marlene comes back.

JOAN	I didn't live a woman's life. I don't understand it.
GRISELDA	The girl was sixteen and far more beautiful than me. I could see why he loved her. / She had her younger brother with her as a page.

The Waltress enters.

MARLENE	Oh God, I can't bear it. I want some coffee. Six coffees. Six brandies. / Double brandies. Straightaway.
GRISELDA	They all went in to the feast I'd prepared. And he stayed behind and put his arms round me and kissed me. / I felt half asleep with the shock.

170

NIJO	Oh, like a dream.
MARLENE	And he said, 'This is your daughter and your son.'

GRISELDA   Yes.

JOAN   What?

NIJO   Oh. Oh I see. You got them back.

ISABELLA   I did think it was remarkably barbaric to kill them but you learn not to say anything. / So he had them brought up secretly, I suppose.   180

MARLENE   Walter's a monster. Weren't you angry? What did you do?

GRISELDA   Well, I fainted. Then I cried and kissed the children. / Everyone was making a fuss of me.

NIJO   But did you feel anything for them?

GRISELDA   What?

NIJO   Did you feel anything for the children?

GRISELDA   Of course, I loved them.

JOAN   So you forgave him and lived with him?

GRISELDA   He suffered so much all those years.   190

ISABELLA   Hennie had the same sweet nature.

NIJO   So they dressed you again?

GRISELDA   Cloth of gold.

JOAN   I can't forgive anything.

MARLENE   You really are exceptional, Griselda.

NIJO   Nobody gave me back my children.

D5: Volpone

Writer: Ben Jonson

Date: 1605

Staging: *Volpone* was probably first performed in the Globe (Shakespeare and Jonson were close friends), and later in the Blackfriars, an indoor theatre also owned by Shakespeare's company, built inside a large hall not far from St Paul's Cathedral.

The story so far

Volpone is extremely rich and, because he has no family, the greedy inhabitants of Venice are constantly visiting him in the hope of inheriting his money. Volpone (Italian for 'fox') is aware of what they are doing and has his own plans. Aided by his servant Mosca (the 'fly'), he pretends to be so ill that he is on the point of death. The greedy neighbours flock to his house, all bringing rich gifts. Mosca tells each one in turn that Volpone is so grateful for their presents, that he has left them all his wealth – and that the time of his death is fast approaching.

Day by day, they bring more and more bribes and the cunning Mosca deceives them brilliantly. One of the visitors is a lawyer called Corvino ('crow'), a rich merchant with a beautiful young wife. In this scene, quite near the opening of the play, Mosca has just got rid of one visitor, when there is a knock on the door, and Corvino arrives.

Another knocks . . .

VOLPONE	Who's that, there, now? a third?
MOSCA	Close, to your couch again; I hear his voice. It is Corvino, our spruce merchant.
VOLPONE	*(lying down)* Dead.
MOSCA	**Another bout**, sir, with your eyes. Who's there?

Enter Corvino.

Another bout   Mosca applies more ointment.

MOSCA	Signior Corvino! come most wished for! O,
	How happy were you, if you knew it, now!
CORVINO	Why? what? wherein?
MOSCA	The tardy hour is come, sir.
CORVINO	He is not dead?
MOSCA	Not dead, sir, but as good;
	He knows no man
CORVINO	How shall I do, then?
MOSCA	Why, sir?
CORVINO	I have brought him, here, a pearl.
MOSCA	Perhaps he has
	So much remembrance left, as to know you, sir;
	He still calls on you, nothing but your name
	Is in his mouth; is your pearl **orient**, sir?
CORVINO	Venice was never owner of the like.
VOLPONE	*(faintly)* Signior Corvino.
MOSCA	Hark.
VOLPONE	Signior Corvino.
MOSCA	He calls you, step and give it him. He's here, sir.
	And he has brought you a rich pearl.
CORVINO	How do you do, sir?
	Tell him it doubles the twelfth **carat**,
MOSCA	Sir,
	He cannot understand, his hearing's gone;
	And yet it comforts him, to see you –
CORVINO	Say,
	I have a **diamant** for him, too.
MOSCA	Best show't, sir,

---

orient eastern pearls were of a superior value and brilliancy.
carat measure of weight of precious stones.
diamant diamond.

Put it into his hand; 'tis only there
He apprehends: he has his feeling, yet

Volpone seizes the pearl.

See how he grasps it!

CORVINO   'Las, good gentleman!
How pitiful the sight is!

MOSCA   Tut, forget, sir.
The weeping of an heir should still be laughter,
Under a visor.

CORVINO   Why? am I his heir?

MOSCA   Sir, I am sworn, I may not show the will,
Till he be dead: but, here has been Corbaccio,
Here has been Voltore, here were others too,
I cannot number 'em, they were so many,
All gaping here for legacies, but I,
Taking the vantage of his naming you,
'**Signior Corvino**, Signior Corvino', took
Paper, and pen, and ink, and there I asked him,
Whom he would have his heir? 'Corvino'. Who
Should be executor? 'Corvino'. And
To any question he was silent to,
I still interpreted the nods he made,
Through weakness, for consent; and sent home
        th'others,
Nothing bequeathed them, but to cry, and curse.

They embrace.

CORVINO   O, my dear Mosca. Does he not perceive us?

The weeping . . . visor Mosca is making the point that, although an heir ought to
appear to be sad at a man's death, he will be laughing inwardly if he knows he's going
to inherit the man's money.
visor a mask.
Signior Corvino Mosca mimics Volpone's feeble cry.

MOSCA	No more than a **blind harper**. He knows no man,

MOSCA   No more than a **blind harper**. He knows no man,
No face of friend, nor name of any servant,
Who 'twas that fed him last, or gave him drink:
Not those, he hath begotten, or brought up
Can he remember.

CORVINO   Has he children?

MOSCA   Bastards,
Some dozen, or more, that he begot on beggars,
Gipsies, and Jews, and black-moors, when he was drunk.
Knew you not that, sir? 'Tis the common **fable**,
The Dwarf, the Fool, the Eunuch are all his;
He's the true father of his **family**,
In all, save me: but he has given 'em nothing.

CORVINO   That's well, that's well. Art sure he does not hear us?

MOSCA   Sure, sir? Why, look you, credit your own sense.

Shouts in Volpone's ear.

The **pox** approach, and add to your diseases,
If it would send you hence the sooner, sir,
For, your incontinence, it hath deserved it
Throughly and throughly, and the plague to boot.
(To Corvino) You may come near, sir.
                         Would you once close
Those filthy eyes of yours, that flow with slime,
Like two frog-pits; and those same hanging cheeks
Covered with hide instead of skin – Nay, help, sir –
That look like frozen dish-clouts, set on end.

CORVINO   Or, like an old smoked wall, on which the rain
Ran down in streaks.

---

blind harper an anonymous busker in a crowd.
fable story, report (not 'fiction').
family household.
pox syphilis, a sexually transmitted disease.

MOSCA	Excellent, sir, speak out;

MOSCA   Excellent, sir, speak out;
You may be louder yet; a **culverin**
Discharged in his ear, would hardly bore it.

CORVINO   His nose is like a common sewer, still running.

MOSCA   'Tis good! And what his mouth?

CORVINO   A very **draught**.

MOSCA   O, stop it up – *(Starts to smother him.)*

CORVINO   By no means.

MOSCA   Pray you, let me.
Faith, I could stifle him, **rarely**, with a pillow,
As well as any woman that should **keep** him.

CORVINO   Do as you will, but I'll be gone.

MOSCA   Be so;
It is your presence makes him last so long.

CORVINO   I pray you, use no violence.

MOSCA   No, sir? why?
Why should you be thus scrupulous, pray you, sir?

CORVINO   Nay, at your discretion.

MOSCA   Well, good sir, be gone.

CORVINO   I will not trouble him now, to take my **pearl**?

MOSCA   Puh! nor your diamant. What a needless care
Is this afflicts you! *(Takes the jewels.)* Is not all, here, yours?
Am not I here? whom you have made? your creature?
That owe my being to you?

CORVINO   Grateful Mosca!
Thou art my friend, my fellow, my companion,

---

culverin hand-gun.
draught sink, cesspool.
rarely excellently.
keep keep house for, look after.
pearl this, with the diamond, is still in Volpone's fist.

	My partner, and shalt share in all my fortunes.
MOSCA	Excepting one.
CORVINO	What's that?
MOSCA	Your **gallant** wife, sir.

Exit Corvino.

Now, is he gone; we had no other means
To shoot him hence, but this.

| VOLPONE | My divine Mosca! |

Thou hast today outgone thyself.

Another knocks.

Who's there?
I will be troubled with no more. Prepare
Me music, dances, banquets, all delights;
The Turk is not more sensual in his pleasures
Than will Volpone.

Exit Mosca.

Let me see, a pearl!
A diamant! plate! **chequeens**! Good morning's
    purchase;
Why, this is better than rob churches, yet;
Or fat, by eating, once a month, a man.

---

gallant fine, beautiful.
chequeens gold coins.
purchase haul; takings (thieves' slang).

Activities: Section D: Viewpoints on Society

D1: An Inspector Calls, page 142.

1   In groups of four, make notes on the very different attitudes and viewpoints of Mr Birling, the Inspector and Sheila, when they are discussing Eva Smith's experiences and the part they have played in her life. Then pick out two or three sections from the extracts which clearly show these differences and perform them in a way that will bring the differences out.

2   At the end of the play, the Inspector says 'We are all responsible for one another.' Look through the extract and note down the points at which this idea of 'responsibility' arises.

   • In what ways are Birling and Sheila responsible for Eva Smith's downfall?

   • How does the play show that a) the poor have no power; and b) powerful people should not merely think of themselves?

3   Write a short article for the local paper about Eva Smith's death. Add some comments about the involvement of Birling and Sheila, with quotes from each one, taken from the extract.

D2: I Will Marry When I Want, page 148.

1   Read the extract in groups of three and then discuss what you have learnt about the society that Gathoni and her parents come from and the conditions in which they live. What do their main concerns seem to be?

2   Gathoni's parents use proverbs to get ideas across and make statements about the world. For example, Wangeci says 'A fool's walking stick supports the clever'. What does she mean by that?

   • Make a list of the other proverbs and write down what the characters mean by them.

3   Write an extract from a scene similar to this one, but set in your
    own society, in which parents complain about 'young people these
    days'.

D3: Sizwe Bansi is Dead, page 153.

1   In pairs, rehearse the extract and then discuss exactly why Sizwe
    is so reluctant to become Robert Zwelinzima. What is he afraid of
    losing? Then act it out again, showing how Buntu manages to
    overcome Sizwe's reluctance.

2   What does the extract reveal about the system of apartheid at this
    time? In particular, what was the importance of the pass book,
    and how did black people get employment?

3   Sizwe decides that he will take over Robert Zwelinzima's identity.
    Write a scene in which he is stopped and questioned by the
    police. He is asked about his name, address, where he works and
    his NI number. What happens?

D4: Top Girls, page 161.

1   *Top Girls* is written in a very unusual way. To create something that
    sounds like a real conversation, Caryl Churchill has her characters
    interrupt each other.

    • In groups of six, act out a section of the extract from line 105
      ('But you let him take her?') to line 135 ('. . . I would do what he
      said.'). Practise it several times, in order to get the interruptions
      and overlapping speeches right.

    • Afterwards, discuss how difficult it was to perform a script
      written like this and decide how effective it was in making the
      dialogue sound like real speech.

2   In pairs, write a summary of Griselda's story. What impact does it have in a play about women?

3   Write a short scene in the style of *Top Girls*. Use dashes and asterisks as Caryl Churchill does, to mark out where people interrupt or speeches overlap. You could write about a group of people in a café or on a bus, with one of them telling a story while the others interrupt and comment.

D5: Volpone, page 169.

1   Rehearse the scene in groups of three. Bring out Volpone's skill in acting the part of a man on the point of death, Mosca's cunning lying and Corvino's greed. Have fun with the section in which Corvino shouts insults at 'the dying man', believing him to be deaf.

2   In your groups, discuss the following questions.

    • Which human vices is Ben Jonson exposing here? (List the vices displayed by Volpone, Mosca and Corvino.)

    • Volpone and Mosca are clearly crooks. But are we on their side? Do we actually want them to get away with their deceptions? Give reasons for your answers.

3   What would the story of Volpone be like if it were written today? Write a modern version of this scene, set in today's world. What would the modern equivalent be of the rich Venetian, Volpone? What kind of wealth would he be hoping to receive from people like Corvino?

Section E: Myth and Morality

Mythology and religion were at the heart of plays from the time of the ancient Greeks through to the Middle Ages and beyond. Two great collections of stories have captured playwrights' imaginations through the ages: the myths of classical Greece and the tales from the Bible.

These lasting stories have enabled audiences from many different backgrounds to see – acted out on stage – emotions, events and situations that human beings have been experiencing since the beginning of time.

E1: Everyman

Writer: not known
Date: some time between 1500 and 1520
Staging: Although some morality plays required mock castles to
be built, or a representation of the entrance to Hell, *Everyman*
could have been performed anywhere, and only needed a simple
platform which could be erected in a village square or a nobleman's
hall.

The story so far

This scene takes place very near to the beginning of this short play.
God, angry that humans are turning their back on him and living
sinfully without fear, tells Death to go to Everyman and inform him
that he must undertake a journey.

God retires. Enter Everyman, finely dressed.

DEATH   Lo, **yonder** I see Everyman walking;
Full little he thinketh on my coming.
His mind is on fleshly **lusts** and his treasure,
And great pain it shall cause him to endure
Before the Lord, Heaven King.

Touches Everyman with his dart.

Everyman, stand still! **Whither art** thou going
Thus gaily? Hast thou **thy maker** forget?

EVERYMAN   Why askest thou?
Wouldest thou wit?

---

yonder over there.
lusts pleasures.
Whither art where are.
thy maker your creator (God).
Wouldest thou wit? Do you want to know?

DEATH	Yea, sir, I will show you.	10
	In great haste I am sent to thee	
	Fro God, out of his majesty	
EVERYMAN	What, sent to me?	
DEATH	**Yea, certainly,**	
	Though thou have forget him here,	
	He thinketh on thee in the heavenly sphere,	
	As, **ere** we depart, thou shalt know.	
EVERYMAN	**What desireth God of me?**	
DEATH	That shall I show thee.	
	A **reckoning** he will needs have,	20
	Without any longer **respite**.	
EVERYMAN	To give a reckoning **longer leisure I crave**.	
	This blind matter troubleth my wit.	
DEATH	On thee thou must take a long journey;	
	Therefore thy **book of count** with thee thou bring,	
	For turn again thou cannot by no way.	
	And look thou be sure of thy reckoning,	
	For before God thou shalt answer and show	
	Thy many bad deeds, and good but a few,	
	How thou hast spent thy life, and in what **wise**,	30
	Before the **chief Lord of paradise**.	
	Have ado that we were in that way,	
	For, wit thou well, thou shalt make none attorney.	

Yea, certainly Yes, indeed.

ere before.

What desireth . . . What does God want of me?

reckoning account; record (of your life and deeds).

respite delay.

longer leisure I crave I need more time.

book of count accounts book.

wise way; manner.

chief Lord of paradise God.

Have ado . . . **attorney** Get ready, because you had better understand that you won't be able to take a lawyer with you.

EVERYMAN	Full unready I am such reckoning to give.
	I know thee not. What messenger art thou?
DEATH	I am Death, that no man **dreadeth**,
	For every man I rest, and no man spareth,
	For it is God's commandment
	That all to me should be obedient.
EVERYMAN	O Death, thou comest when I had thee least in mind! 40
	In thy power it **lieth** me to save.
	Yet of my good will I give thee, if thou will be kind –
	Yea, a thousand pound shalt thou have,
	And **defer** this matter till another day.
DEATH	Everyman, it may not be, by no way.
	I set not by gold, silver, nor **richesse**,
	Ne by pope, emperor, king, duke, ne princess.
	For, and I would receive gifts great,
	All the world I might get.
	But my custom is clean contrary. 50
	I give thee no respite. Come **hence**, and not **tarry**.
EVERYMAN	Alas, shall I have no longer respite?
	I may say, 'Death giveth no warning!'
	To think on thee it maketh my heart sick,
	For all unready is my book of reckoning.
	But twelve year and I might have abiding,
	My counting-book I would make so clear
	That my reckoning I should not need to fear.
	Wherefore, Death, I pray thee, for God's mercy.
	Spare me till I be provided of remedy. 60

---

dreadeth fears.
lieth lies.
defer put off.
richesse riches, wealth.
Ne nor.
hence here.
tarry hang about; delay.
But twelve . . . abiding If I could be allowed to wait twelve years.

DEATH	**Thee availeth not to cry**, weep, and pray;
	But haste thee lightly that thou were gone that journey,
	And prove thy friends if thou can,
	For, wit thou well, the tide abideth no man,
	And in the world each living creature
	For Adam's sin must die of nature.
EVERYMAN	Death, if I should this pilgrimage take,
	And my reckoning surely make,
	Show me, for saint charity,
	Should I not **come again** shortly?
DEATH	No, Everyman; and thou be once there,
	Thou mayst never more come here,
	Trust me **verily**.
EVERYMAN	O gracious God in the high seat celestial,
	Have mercy on me in this most need!
	Shall I have no company fro this **vale terrestrial**
	Of mine acquaintance, that way me to lead?
DEATH	Yea, if any be so **hardy**
	That would go with thee and bear thee company.

70

Thee availeth not to cry It's no good crying.
come again return; come back.
verily truly.
vale terrestrial here, on Earth.
hardy bold.

E2: The Odyssey

Writer: Derek Walcott, based upon the ancient Greek epic poem by Homer.
Date: The original epic poem was possibly written in the eighth century BCE. Derek Walcott wrote this version in 1993.
Staging: A completely empty space. The actors, in the costumes of figures from Greek mythology, bring on any props they need to set each scene.

The story so far

After ten years, the Greek army has finally succeeded in defeating Troy and burning the city to the ground. But there has been a heavy cost to pay, and Achilles, their greatest warrior hero, is dead. A singer introduces the story. Then, as the play opens, the Greek leaders throw weapons onto Achilles's funeral pyre.

Scene 1

Troy. Dusk. Heavy smoke. The kings, Agamemnon, Menelaus and Nestor, with Ajax and Thersites, the mercenary, pile weapons on a pyre. Drums.

AGAMEMNON	Pile our worn weapons on this remembering **cairn**.
NESTOR	Till salt air rusts them, till they're wrapped in veils of sand.
MENELAUS	Turn the gaping beaks of our fleet homeward again.
AJAX	Since Troy is a plain of ashes where **kites** ascend.
THERSITES	Till men ask 'Was it here?' of the gliding **frigate**.
AGAMEMNON	'Was it here that their lances pinned Achilles' pyre?'
NESTOR	Who rattles his angry lance along heaven's gate.

---

cairn pile of rocks set up as a monument.
kites scavenger birds.
frigate large bird of prey.

AGAMEMNON	Through the length of war, home was our long desire.
MENELAUS	It was mine, Menelaus, whose wife was its cause.
AJAX	And mine, Ajax, the heir of Achilles' armour.

Odysseus enters at a distance.

ODYSSEUS	What?
THERSITES	Not mine, Thersites. No wife, no son, no house.
AGAMEMNON	And ingenious Odysseus.
NESTOR	And mine, Nestor.

Pause. A swallow twitters overhead. They look up.

MENELAUS	That swallow's eager to leave. Where's Odysseus?
THERSITES	In his tent, checking his tribute.
AJAX	Once more, we wait.

Odysseus steps forward, eating.

AGAMEMNON	We're piling gifts on Achilles' mound. Any size.

Odysseus pays his small tribute.

ODYSSEUS	There. I couldn't choose what to give. Sorry I'm late.

Silence.

O lucky dead, who can't tell friends from enemies!

Silence.

Agamemnon denied you flame-haired **Briseis**.

Silence.

Menelaus mocked you: 'Deliverer from Mice'.

Briseis slave-girl taken from Achilles by Agamemnon.

Silence.

Now all your glories are reflected in their eyes.

NESTOR   This scrolled shield **Hephaestus** hammered, who is
its heir?

He holds up a shield.

THERSITES   He willed it to Odysseus on the battlefield.

AJAX   Achilles was fitful. He promised me first.

ODYSSEUS   Where?

AJAX   Look, two claims injure his spirit! You take the
shield.

ODYSSEUS   No, no, you take it, Ajax, you fought the hardest.

AJAX   You heard me say that? Did I ever make that boast?

MENELAUS   For God's sake, it's his burial mound. Let him rest.

He gives Odysseus the shield.

AJAX   Bear it, you turtle! Take ten years to reach your
coast.

AGAMEMNON   Now let the coiled rams' horns moan with our
departure.

MENELAUS   Let the eagle's **pennon** steer us through the
cloud's foam.

Horns and drums.

AGAMEMNON   Let these pennons tatter after ten years of war.

NESTOR   Let wet-heeled **Athena** race our lunging ships
home.

Hephaestus the armourer of the gods.

pennon long, narrow flag; standard.

Athena the goddess of war and wisdom, who supported the Greeks.

E3: Tales from Ovid

Writer: The original stories were written in Latin by the Roman poet, Ovid. Ted Hughes turned them into English poetry and the poem was then adapted for the stage by Tim Supple and Simon Reade.
Date: The play version was created in 1999.
Staging: The play was first performed at the Royal Shakespeare Company's Swan Theatre, Stratford-upon-Avon. The stage was covered in sand and the actors wore costumes based on drawings seen on ancient Greek vases. Music, often provided by percussion and a Greek lyre (a kind of harp), accompanied a lot of the action and dialogue.

The story so far
The play is in ten sections, each one based on one of the myths in which people are turned into other things: Narcissus into a flower, for example, or Arachne into a spider. In this final section, the foolish King Midas declares that the music of the goat-god Pan is better than the music of the great god Apollo. His punishment is swift and dramatic!

(BACCHUS)   Apollo's face seemed to **writhe**
                Momentarily
                As he converted this clown's darkness to light,

(APOLLO)   Then he pointed his **plectrum** at the ears
                That had misheard so grievously.

(BACCHUS)   Abruptly those ears **lolled** long and animal,
                On either side of King Midas' impertinent face –
                Grey-whiskered, bristly,
                The familiar ears of a big ass.

---

writhe contort, twist with emotion.
plectrum small instrument of ivory, etc. for plucking strings.
lolled flopped.

(MIDAS)	*(grabs his new ears)* Then he had some seconds of pure terror
	Waiting for the rest of his body to follow.
(APOLLO)	But this was the god's decision: Midas
	Lived on, human, wagging the ears of a donkey.
(MIDAS)	Midas crept away.
	Every few paces he felt at his ears and groaned.
	He slunk back to his palace. He needed
	Comfort. He was bitterly disillusioned
	With the spirit of the wilderness.
	He hid those ears – in a turban superb
	As compensation could be.
(BARBER)	But a king needs a barber.
	Sworn to secrecy or **impalement**,
	The barber, wetting his lips,
	Clipped around the gristly roots
	Of the great angling ears as if the hair there
	Might be live nerve-ends.
	What he was staring at,
	And having to believe, was worse
	For him than for their owner,
	Almost. He had to hide this news
	As if it were red-hot
	Under his tongue, and keep it there.
	The ultimate shame-secret
	Of the ruler of the land.
	It struggled to blurt
	Itself out, whenever
	He opened his mouth.
	It made him sweat and often
	Gasp aloud, or strangle
	A groan to a sigh. Or wake up

---

impalement being skewered on a sharp pole.

In the middle of the silent night
Certain he had just
Yelled it out, at the top of his voice,
To the whole city.
He knew
He had to spit it out somehow.

In the lawn of a park he lifted a turf
After midnight. He kneeled there
And whispered into the raw hole:

BARBER   Ass's ears! Midas has ass's ears!

(BARBER)   Then he fitted the turf back, trod flat the grave
Of that **insuppressible** gossip,
And went off, singing
Under his breath.

(REEDS)   But in no time,
A clump of reeds bunched out.
It looked strange, on the park lawn,
But sounded stranger.
Every gust brought an **inarticulate** whisper
Out of the bending stalks. At every puff
They betrayed the barber's confidence,
Broadcasting the buried secret:

REEDS   *(hissing)* Ass's ears! Ass's ears! Midas has ass's ears!
Ass's ears! Midas has ass's ears!

---

insuppressible impossible to keep quiet.
inarticulate in words difficult at first to understand.

Activities: Section E, Myth and Morality

E1: Everyman, page 180.

1   *Everyman* was written for a Christian audience who believed that a
    human being's soul would go to be judged by God after the death
    of the body. As the play develops, Everyman goes around to all his
    friends, asking which of them will accompany him on his journey
    with Death. The first friends he approaches are called Fellowship,
    Kindred (and Cousin), Goods and Good Deeds.

    • Discuss what you think each of these characters represents.
    • One of them says to Everyman:
      'Everyman, I will go with thee and be thy guide,
      In thy most need to go by thy side.'

    Discuss which one is most likely to say this, and give reasons for
    your decision.

2   *Everyman* was written about six centuries ago and the language
    has changed a great deal in that time.

    • Use the footnotes to check the meanings of these words and
      phrases, which are not usually heard in modern Standard
      English:
          'Wouldest thou wit' (line 9)
          'ere we depart' (line 17)
          'in what wise' (line 30)
          'Come hence and not tarry' (line 51)
          'Thee availeth not to cry' (line 61)

    • What words and phrases do the characters use instead of 'Why
      do you ask?' (line 8), 'Before we leave' (17) and 'truly' (73)?
    • Write your own version, in modern everyday English, of lines
      24–31 ('On thee thou must . . . Lord of paradise.').

3   Write your version of the scene in which Everyman asks one of his
    friends (Fellowship, Kindred and Cousin, Goods or Good Deeds) to
    accompany him on his journey. Think carefully about how this

particular friend will reply. When you make up the scene, you can either copy the style of the original or write in modern English.

E2: The Odyssey, page 184.

1   Although it isn't obvious at first, the dialogue is in rhyming verse. Perform the extract in groups of six, bringing out the rhymes and half-rhymes.

2   Derek Walcott's play picks up the Troy story more than ten years after Agamemnon sacrificed his daughter in order to get a fair wind (see *The Agamemnon* on pages 110–13). In your groups, discuss the following questions:

- What do the leaders feel about their victory?
- What does Ajax think of Odysseus? How can you tell?
- What do you notice about Odysseus's tribute? What does that seem to suggest?
- What does Odysseus feel about Achilles's glories and successes now that he is dead?
- Ajax utters a curse, which comes true later on. What does he say and what will happen?

3   Imagine you were directing this play.

- Re-read the extract including the opening stage directions, and sketch what the set ought to look like.
- Then write notes on how the actors ought to perform the scene. What actions would be effective? How should they deliver the lines?

E3: Tales from Ovid, page 187.

1   In the script, the characters also act as narrators. For example, the Barber says 'Ass's ears! Midas has ass's ears!', but he also goes on to tell the story of what then happened: 'Then he fitted the turf back ...' You can tell which are the narrative sections, because

the characters' names are in brackets. Read the extract in groups of four. In particular, practise saying the final two lines altogether so that they sound like the whispering of reeds in the breeze.

2   In the same groups, create freeze-frames to represent the key moments. You could show the point at which

- Apollo punishes Midas
- Midas first reveals his ears to the barber
- the barber speaks his secret into the ground
- the reeds spring up to whisper it to the air.

Decide how you can most simply and effectively represent this final scene.

3   Write a playscript for another myth (or part of one) in this style. Use the characters as narrators and stage the scenes as simply as you can. You could, for example, choose the story from an earlier part of Midas's life, when he makes a wish that everything he touches will turn to gold.

Section F: Mystery and Suspense

Mystery and suspense are things that we most obviously associate with films or television. But they have always been a central part of stage plays, and there is something particularly exciting about a tense and gripping scene acted out in front of a 'live' audience.

Suspense can be created in a number of ways. Sometimes, as in *Macbeth*, we know exactly what has happened, but we experience the characters' growing panic. In other plays, the fear comes from something unknown, or the doubt in our mind about exactly what is going to happen, and when . . .

F1: Sherlock Holmes and the Limehouse Horror

Writer: Philip Pullman, based upon the stories written by Sir Arthur Conan Doyle, between 1887 and 1902.

Date: 1985

Staging: Realistic sets and costumes. This version was first performed at the Polka Children's Theatre, Wimbledon.

The story so far

The scene takes place in a warehouse. The villain Reichenbach has secretly brought into the country a monstrous creature – the notorious 'giant rat of Sumatra' – referred to in another Sherlock Holmes story. He explains his plans to Sir Henry Murray, who realises that he has become involved with a madman.

Neither of them has yet noticed that an old tramp has found his way into the warehouse and is asleep in the corner . . .

SIR HENRY	Oh, dear God – what have I got into? You're mad, Reichenbach! Insane!
REICHENBACH	Oh, I don't think so. I am conscious of a peculiar clarity of mind.
SIR HENRY	But . . . What of the rat? It must be fed, it must be taken out of here as soon as possible. You said you'd make arrangements. What's going to happen?
REICHENBACH	The rat stays here.
SIR HENRY	But – but – the breeding programme! We agreed! My female, and this new male – this is an unparalleled opportunity! Do you mean me to bring the female here?
REICHENBACH	You may do as you please – afterwards.
SIR HENRY	Afterwards?

10

REICHENBACH	I have a purpose of my own for this creature. Why else do you think I would have agreed to finance this expedition? For the pure love of science?
SIR HENRY	But – but what else is there?
REICHENBACH	If I told you, Murray, you would not believe it.
SIR HENRY	Does it involve danger to the rat?
REICHENBACH	Danger? What in the world could threaten a creature like that? I saw a cat downstairs – are you worried about that? Fool! The rat would snap it up like a fly. Open the cage!
SIR HENRY	What – now?
REICHENBACH	Open it, I say!
SIR HENRY	But – but – have you seen the rat move, Reichenbach?
REICHENBACH	I hope to very soon.
SIR HENRY	It's asleep now, but when it wakes, it moves with the speed of a leopard. Terrifying . . . Please, Reichenbach, let us get out and –

He stops suddenly and points into the corner. He has seen the Tramp.

Look!

REICHENBACH	How long has he been here?
SIR HENRY	I didn't see him come in . . .

He stirs the Tramp urgently with his foot.

Wake up! What are you doing here? Get out! Get out at once!

The Tramp cringes and scuttles away.

20

30

TRAMP	Beg pardon, sir – no offence – poor old man 40 looking for shelter on a raw night – pity the poor old soldier, sir . . .

He whines and cringes.

REICHENBACH	You have nowhere else to go?
TRAMP	Nowhere in the world, sir –
REICHENBACH	Does anyone know you're here?
TRAMP	No one knows and no one cares. I fought for me country in the Crimea, sir – four months in the snow – lost four toes with frostbite – look, sir, look –

He offers to show them his revolting foot. They decline.

REICHENBACH	You're perfectly alone in the world? No relations? 50
TRAMP	Not a one in the world, sir – me daughter's gorn to Heaven and took her babe with her, me little grandchild as used to sit on me knee . . . All gone now. I got no one left . . .

He snivels and sips furtively at his flask. Reichenbach draws Murray aside.

REICHENBACH	Perfect! Perfect! When did the rat last eat?
SIR HENRY	This morning . . . But surely! You don't mean –

They both look round at the Tramp.

REICHENBACH	Who will ever know? You heard him – he's completely alone in the world! A worthless old tramp – no one knows he's here!
SIR HENRY	I can't do it. Reichenbach, this is a human being! 60
REICHENBACH	What does that matter? Think of the rat, Murray! Think of its offspring. A family, a tribe, a population of them! Your female and this male –

and what can his life mean to this wretched old
fellow? A weary shuffle from day to day, begging a
living, sleeping in corners to keep out of the
workhouse – hungry, cold, miserable – it'll be a
merciful release.

SIR HENRY   I – I – oh, get it over with. This business sickens me.

Reichenbach turns to the Tramp.

REICHENBACH   You're an old soldier, you say?   70

TRAMP   Colour-Sergeant, sir. 49th Dragoons. Served me
country in the Crimea –

REICHENBACH   Yes, yes. Well, we don't want to turn a gallant old
soldier out into the night. You stay here, and make
the best of it. How's that flask?

*The Tramp can hardly believe his luck. He holds out the
flask and Reichenbach fills it from one of his own.*

A drop of brandy to keep out the cold Sleep well,
Colour-Sergeant!

The Tramp stands erect and salutes.

TRAMP   Good night to you, sir! God bless you for a
fine gentleman!

SIR HENRY   Come on, Reichenbach.   80

The Tramp settles down to sleep.

REICHENBACH   Open the cage, Murray.

*Sir Henry reluctantly opens wide the door at the centre.
Through it we can see dimly a stout wooden box the
height of a tall man and eight feet or so broad.*

*Sir Henry unfastens some bolts and pulls away the front
of the box, to reveal a steel cage. Inside it, something
huge and dark is sleeping.*

Reichenbach holds the lantern high and looks through the doorway at it.

REICHENBACH   Formidable! Magnificent! The sheer size . . .

Sir Henry opens the door of the cage. There is nothing now to keep the rat from getting out. Taking care not to make too much noise. Sir Henry tiptoes back into the main room, leaving the door ajar. We can't see the rat, but we know it's there.

SIR HENRY   Come on – it's stirring. It won't be long before it wakes.

REICHENBACH   We'll go up to the next floor – and wait.

They go out. The Tramp stirs briefly, then settles again.

Pause.

We hear a cab drawing up. The outside door opens, and echoes around the building, as before. The crack of a whip, and the cab drives away.

Footsteps creak up the stairs. The door opens. A figure with a lantern comes in – bowler-hatted, overcoated. He holds up the lantern, and we see that it is Dr Watson.

WATSON   Place is empty. I wonder where he can be?

He looks round and sees the Tramp. He starts with surprise.

Good grief!

He looks closer.

Oh, he's only asleep . . . An old tramp.

Suddenly the Tramp wakes up and starts away. Watson jumps.

TRAMP	It's all right, sir – beg pardon, sir – no offence – poor old soldier, sir –

90

WATSON	Quiet, man! How long have you been here?
TRAMP	Not long, sir – on me life, sir! I got permission –
WATSON	Keep your voice down!

He looks around apprehensively.

Have you seen a gentleman come in here in the past half hour?

TRAMP	No, sir – been on watch, sir – night watchman, that's me. You didn't ought to be here. This is private property, this is.
WATSON	Night watchman? Don't be absurd. You're in great danger here, and you must leave at once.

100

TRAMP	Danger, sir?
WATSON	Terrible danger. Take your belongings and go at once. Here – *(He takes out a coin.)* Find yourself a bed for the night. But don't stay here.

The Tramp takes the coin, then stands up.

TRAMP	Watson, you're a splendid fellow – which is why I forgive you for being such an ass.

He sweeps off the grey wig. It is Holmes. Watson is amazed.

WATSON	Holmes! My dear fellow – but why the disguise?
HOLMES	We're up against something devilish here, Watson. The rat is loose – and I'm the bait for it. I told you to stay away.

110

WATSON	What, and leave you here alone? Never!
HOLMES	I wanted you in Baker Street, Watson. There's a job to be done there –

WATSON	But the danger! Holmes, my place is at your side. What could I do in Baker Street?
HOLMES	The most vital task of all. Watson, if I die –
WATSON	Hush! What's that?

A sporadic swishing sound can be heard, as of a giant tail sweeping the floor of a cage.

HOLMES	The rat's awake! Are you armed, Watson?
WATSON	Of course –
HOLMES	Then stay here – and defend yourself!	120

He runs to the door, pauses a second, then rushes through, pulling it shut after him.

WATSON	Holmes! What are you doing? Come back!

He runs to the door, pulling a pistol from his pocket.

Holmes! Wait for me –

Suddenly there is a wild animal shriek, and a hideous snarling.

Watson hammers on the door, which he cannot open.

Holmes! Open the door!

Various appalling noises come from behind the door – climaxed by a wild cry in Holmes's voice.

F2: The Woman in Black

Writer: Stephen Mallatratt (based on the novel by Susan Hill)
Date: 1991
Staging: The stage set is itself designed to represent a stage, as the action takes place in a deserted theatre (or in our imaginations, as the actors perform the story). Lighting and sound effects are extremely important.

The story so far

Kipps has written up the story of a terrifying experience he once had, and which still haunts him. He has approached a professional actor, because he wants some practice in reading his story out loud. He thinks that, if he can read the account to a small group of friends, it will help him to get over the experience.

The actor agrees to help and, day by day, becomes more and more involved in Kipps's strange and disturbing tale.

At this point in the play, the two men are acting out a moment when Kipps, as a young lawyer, has been sent to a remote coastal village to sort out the papers of an old woman who has just died, a Mrs Drablow.

But Kipps finds that no one wants to accompany him to Eel Marsh House, where the old lady lived, and he thinks he has discovered why. In this scene, he is talking to a local man, Sam Daily, about a ghostly figure that he has seen.

KIPPS   . . . It seems to me, Mr Daily, that I have seen whatever ghost haunts Eel Marsh. A woman in black with a wasted face. Because I have no doubt at all that she was what people call a ghost, that she was not a real, living, breathing, human being. Well, she did me no harm. She neither spoke nor came near me. I did not like her look and I like the – the power that seemed to **emanate from**

---

emanate from   come out from; issue from.

her towards me even less, but I have convinced myself that it is a power that cannot do more than make me feel afraid. If I go there and see her again, I am prepared. 10

SAM DAILY And the pony and trap?

Silence.

KIPPS So you know of that. *(At length)* I won't run away.

SAM DAILY You shouldn't go there.

KIPPS I'm afraid I'm going.

SAM DAILY You shouldn't go there alone.

KIPPS It seems I can find no one to come with me.

SAM DAILY No. And you will not.

KIPPS Good God, man, Mrs Drablow lived alone there for – what was it? – sixty odd years, to a ripe old age. She 20 must have come to terms with all the ghosts about the place.

SAM DAILY Ay. Maybe that's just what she did do. *(Pause.)* But you're set on it?

KIPPS I am.

SAM DAILY Then take a dog.

KIPPS *(laughing)* I haven't got a dog.

SAM DAILY I have. *(He whistles, then bends and pats the 'dog'.)* Take her. Bring her back when you are done.

KIPPS Will she come with me? 30

SAM DAILY She'll do what I tell her.

Kipps pets her.

KIPPS What's her name?

SAM DAILY Spider.

KIPPS   All right, I'll be glad of her company, I confess. Thank
        you. Come, girl! Spider!

        Kipps and the 'dog' move out of the light.

ACTOR   *(loosening his 'Daily' clothes)* Next morning, he crosses
        to the house on a bicycle lent him by his landlord.
        The little dog Spider bounds behind. The sun is high,
        the very air seems purified and more exhilarating.

KIPPS   There they lay, those glittering, beckoning, silver   40
        marshes. I could hear the mysterious silence, and
        once again the haunting, strange beauty of it all
        aroused a response deep within me. I could not run
        away from that place. I had fallen under some sort of
        spell of the kind that certain places **exude** and it drew
        me, my imaginings, my longings, my curiosity, my
        whole spirit, towards itself.

        *The lights suggest the house interior. The Actor moves to
        the side of the stage, to a position as physically removed
        from Kipps as possible – perhaps even to the body of the
        theatre.*

ACTOR   He lights fires, airs sheets and blankets, opens
        windows, draws up blinds, and sets himself to work
        in one of the bays of the morning-room.   50

        *Kipps starts sorting the letters into piles – those to be dealt
        with, those to discard.*

KIPPS   Well, Spider, have you ever seen a more worthless
        collection of papers? I do believe Mrs Drablow kept
        every bill, receipt and Christmas card she ever had.
        (He fondles Spider.) There's even shopping lists, would
        you believe!

---

exude ooze out, give off (like a gas).

ACTOR   It was pretty tedious going, but he persevered patiently enough, untying and cursorily examining bundle after bundle of worthless old papers before tossing them aside.

Kipps works on a moment, then yawns and stretches. He stands, crosses the stage and we hear the door slam. He whistles for the dog.

KIPPS   *(calling)* Spider! Spider – rabbits! *(He moves through the* 60 *gauze into the old graveyard.)* Last time I was here, among these graves, I saw a woman. *(He bends to the dog.)* Where is she, Spider! Where is she, girl! *(He pats the dog, then stoops to decipher an inscription.)* In Loving Memory . . . Something net . . . Humfrye . . . nineteen o-something . . . and of her something . . . iel Drablow . . . *(He contemplates the stone a moment, then whistles the dog.)* Spider!

ACTOR   He returns to the house and to his task. Already the air is turning colder, the sky losing its light.   70

We hear the door slam as Kipps returns to his papers.

On into the evening he works. Spider is an excellent companion and he is glad of her gentle breathing, her occasional scratching or clattering about in that big empty house. But his main sensation is one of tedium and a certain lethargy, combined with a desire to finish the job and be back in London with his dear Stella.

Kipps sorts through the papers, discarding many, saving few, as the lights fade. When they return, he is in the process of clearing his work for the night, putting things in piles on the floor.

---

gauze the sheet of see-through material on stage.

KIPPS   Another day or two and we'll be done. it's time for
bed. Come, Spider!

*He moves by a **circuitous** route to his bed. He lies down,
covering himself with a blanket he has found amongst the
clutter. Before the lights go down, he reaches down to
fondle the dog.*

Would Mr Daily let me take you home with me to   80
London? I wonder. You'd like Stella. I'm not sure
you'd like London. Good-night now. Good-night.

*And the lights fade to a black-out. Suddenly, they return,
via a shaft of moonlight, and Kipps sits immediately
upright. Silence.*

(At length, whispering) What is it, Spider? What is it?

*Silence. Then, from the depths of the house, comes a sound
like an intermittent bump or rumble. Kipps listens, frozen.
At length, it stops. Slowly, he climbs out of bed.*

(Whispering) Good girl, good girl . . . *(He moves away
from his bed.)*

*The sound begins again. Kipps moves cautiously through
the house. As he does, the moonlight appears and
disappears through the many windows. Gradually, the
sound gets louder as Kipps gets nearer, until, inevitably,
he's drawn to the closed door. The sound is at its loudest
now. Kipps has not the courage to try the door, though it's
evident that the source of the sound is behind it. He stands
as if paralysed outside. Then, from out on the marshes,
comes the sound of a child's cry. Kipps swings around
to listen.*

---

circuitous roundabout.

| ACTOR | He gropes his way back to his bedroom, and looks out. There lie the marshes, silver grey and empty, there is the water of the estuary, flat as a mirror with the full moon lying upturned upon it. |
| KIPPS | But nothing. No one. The slightest of breezes, nothing more. |

90

The distant rumble from the room has now ceased. In silence, Kipps moves back through the house, towards the room with the closed door. He reaches it, there is no sound now. He puts his hand on to the handle, hesitates, then turns it. It does not give. He pushes against it slightly with his shoulder. Nothing. Slowly, the dawn light filters up.

F3: Waiting for Godot

Writer: Samuel Beckett
Date: 1955
Staging: Beckett's introduction to the scene reads: 'A country road. A tree. Evening.' That is all we are given, but in most productions, the tree is dead and without leaves. Apart from that, the stage is bare, except perhaps for a mound or two on which the characters can sit. The two characters are dressed as tramps.

The story so far

This part of the dialogue comes very near the beginning of the play, which opens with one of the tramps, Estragon, trying to take his boot off and giving up exhausted. The other tramp, Vladimir, enters and Estragon says 'Nothing to be done.' They carry on from there.

ESTRAGON	[. . .] *(He turns to Vladimir)* Let's go.
VLADIMIR	We can't.
ESTRAGON	Why not?
VLADIMIR	We're waiting for Godot.
ESTRAGON	*(despairingly)* Ah! *(Pause.)* You're sure it was here?
VLADIMIR	What?
ESTRAGON	That we were to wait.
VLADIMIR	He said by the tree. *(They look at the tree.)* Do you see any others?
ESTRAGON	What is it?
VLADIMIR	I don't know. A willow.
ESTRAGON	Where are the leaves?
VLADIMIR	It must be dead.
ESTRAGON	No more weeping.
VLADIMIR	Or perhaps it's not the season.

ESTRAGON	Looks to me more like a bush.
VLADIMIR	A shrub.
ESTRAGON	A bush.
VLADIMIR	A –. What are you insinuating? That we've come to the wrong place?
ESTRAGON	He should be here.
VLADIMIR	He didn't say for sure he'd come.
ESTRAGON	And if he doesn't come?
VLADIMIR	We'll come back tomorrow.
ESTRAGON	And then the day after tomorrow.
VLADIMIR	Possibly.
ESTRAGON	And so on.
VLADIMIR	The point is –
ESTRAGON	Until he comes.
VLADIMIR	You're merciless.
ESTRAGON	We came here yesterday.
VLADIMIR	Ah no, there you're mistaken.
ESTRAGON	What did we do yesterday?
VLADIMIR	What did we do yesterday?
ESTRAGON	Yes.
VLADIMIR	Why . . . *(Angrily)* Nothing is certain when you're about.
ESTRAGON	In my opinion we were here.
VLADIMIR	*(looking round)* You recognise the place?
ESTRAGON	I didn't say that.
VLADIMIR	Well?
ESTRAGON	That makes no difference.
VLADIMIR	All the same . . . that tree . . . *(Turning towards the auditorium)* . . . that bog.
ESTRAGON	You're sure it was this evening?

VLADIMIR	What?
ESTRAGON	That we were to wait.
VLADIMIR	He said Saturday. *(Pause.)* I think.
ESTRAGON	You think.
VLADIMIR	I must have made a note of it.

He fumbles in his pockets, bursting with miscellaneous rubbish.

ESTRAGON	*(very insidious)* But what Saturday? And is it Saturday? Is it not rather Sunday? *(Pause.)* Or Monday? *(Pause.)* Or Friday?
VLADIMIR	*(looking wildly about him, as though the date was inscribed in the landscape)* It's not possible!
ESTRAGON	Or Thursday?
VLADIMIR	What'll we do?
ESTRAGON	If he came yesterday and we weren't here you may be sure he won't come again today.
VLADIMIR	But you say we were here yesterday.
ESTRAGON	I may be mistaken. *(Pause.)* Let's stop talking for a minute, do you mind?
VLADIMIR	*(feebly)* All right.

F4: Macbeth

Writer: William Shakespeare
Date: 1606
Staging: Macbeth was probably first performed at the Globe, but there were certainly other performances at court.

The story so far

Macbeth and his wife have plotted to kill King Duncan, so that, in line with a prophecy made to him by three witches, Macbeth will himself become king. It is the night of the planned murder, and Macbeth prepares himself to do the deed.

ACT 2

Scene 1

[. . .]

MACBETH Go bid thy mistress, when my drink is ready,
She strike upon **the bell**. Get thee to bed.

Exit Servant.

Is this a dagger which I see before me,
The handle toward my hand? Come let me clutch
 thee.
I have thee not, and yet I see thee still.
Art thou not, fatal vision, sensible
To feeling as to sight? Or art thou but
A dagger of the mind, a false creation,
Proceeding from the **heat-oppressed** brain?
I see thee yet, in form as palpable   10
As this which now I draw.

---

the bell this is the signal for killing Duncan.
heat-oppressed feverish.

Thou marshall'st me the way that I was going,
And such an instrument I was to use.
Mine eyes are made the fools o' th' other senses,
Or else worth all the rest. I see thee still;
And on thy blade and **dudgeon** gouts of blood,
Which was not so before. There's no such thing.
It is the bloody business which informs
Thus to mine eyes. Now o'er the one half-world
Nature seems dead, and wicked dreams abuse   20
The curtained sleep; witchcraft celebrates
Pale **Hecate**'s offerings; and withered murder,
Alarumed by his sentinel the wolf,
Whose howl's his watch, thus with his stealthy pace,
With **Tarquin's** ravishing strides, towards his design
Moves like a ghost. Thou sure and firm-set earth,
Hear not my steps, which way they walk, for fear
Thy very stones **prate of my whereabout**,
And **take the present horror from the time**,
Which now suits with it. Whiles I **threat**, he lives: 30
Words to the heat of deeds too cold breath gives.

A bell rings.

Mine eyes are made the fools . . . either my eyes are stupid compared to the rest of
my senses, or else they are more believable than all the rest.
dudgeon hilt.
It is the bloody . . . eyes the violence of the act is making me see physical shapes in
this way.
Hecate the goddess of witchcraft.
Alarumed called into action.
Tarquin's a Roman who raped (ravished) Lucretia.
prate of my whereabout gossip about where I am going.
take the present horror . . . with it break the horrifying silence which suits what I am
going to do.
threat threaten.
Words to . . . gives words cool down the passion of deeds.

I go, and it is done. The bell invites me.
Hear it not Duncan, for it is a **knell**
That summons thee to heaven or to hell.

Exit.

Scene 2

The same. Enter Lady Macbeth

L. MACBETH   That which hath made them drunk hath made me
        bold;
    What hath quenched them hath given me fire.
        Hark! Peace!
    It was the owl that shrieked, the fatal **bellman**,
    Which gives the stern'st good night. He is **about it**.
    The doors are open; and the **surfeited grooms**
    Do mock their charge with snores. I have drugged
        their **possets**,
    That death and nature do contend about them,
    Whether they live or die.

MACBETH   *(within)*   Who's there? What ho!

L. MACBETH   Alack, I am afraid they have awaked,   10
    And 'tis done. **Th' attempt and not the deed**
    Confounds us. Hark! I laid their daggers ready,

---

knell funeral bell.
What hath . . . the drink which has made them unconscious has given me courage.
bellman the man who rang the bell before an execution.
about it performing the murder.
surfeited grooms . . . charge the drunken serving-men make a mockery of their job
of guarding the king.
possets late-night alcoholic drinks.
Th' attempt . . . us if Macbeth has been caught, we have been ruined by attempting
the killing, rather than actually carrying it out.

He could not miss 'em. Had he he not resembled
My father as he slept, I **had done't.**

Enter Macbeth

                                     My husband!

MACBETH   I have done the deed. Didst thou not hear a noise?

L. MACBETH   I heard the owl scream and the crickets cry.
Did not you speak?

MACBETH   When?

L. MACBETH   Now.

MACBETH   As I descended?

L. MACBETH   Ay.

MACBETH   Hark! Who lies i' th' second chamber?

L. MACBETH   Donalbain.

MACBETH   This is a **sorry** sight. *(Looks on his hands.)*   20

MACBETH   A foolish thought, to say a sorry sight.

MACBETH   There's one did laugh in's sleep, and one cried
       'Murder!'
That they did wake each other. I stood and heard
       them.
But they did say their prayers, and **addressed them**
Again to sleep.

L. MACBETH   There are two **lodged together.**

MACBETH   One cried 'God bless us!' and 'Amen!' the other,
As they had seen me with these hangman's hands.
Listening their fear, I could not say 'Amen',
When they did say 'God bless us!'

I had done't I would have done it myself.
sorry miserable.
That so that.
addressed them got ready.
lodged together sleeping in the same room.
As as if.

L. MACBETH	Consider it not so deeply.

MACBETH But **wherefore** could not I pronounce 'Amen'? 30
I had most need of blessing, and 'Amen'
Stuck in my throat.

L. MACBETH These deeds must not be thought
After these ways; so, it will make us mad.

MACBETH Methought I heard a voice cry 'Sleep no more!
Macbeth does murder sleep,' the innocent sleep,
Sleep that knits up the **ravelled sleave** of care,
The death of each day's life, sore labour's bath,
Balm of hurt minds, great nature's second course,
Chief nourisher in life's feast.

L. MACBETH What do you mean?

MACBETH Still it cried 'Sleep no more!' to all the house. 40
Glamis hath murdered sleep, and therefore Cawdor
Shall sleep no more, **Macbeth shall sleep no more**.

L. MACBETH Who was it that thus cried? **Why worthy Thane**,
You do **unbend** your noble strength, to think
So brainsickly of things. Go get some water,
And wash this **filthy witness** from your hand.
Why did you bring these daggers from the place?
They must lie there. Go carry them, and smear
The sleepy grooms with blood.

MACBETH I'll go no more.
I am afraid to think what I have done. 50
Look on't again I dare not.

---

wherefore why.
After these ways in this way.
ravelled sleave tangled threads.
Balm soothing oil.
Macbeth . . . Thane he is Thane of Glamis and Thane of Cawdor.
unbend weaken.
So brainsickly as though you were delirious.
filthy witness evidence of horrible deeds.

L. MACBETH   Infirm of purpose!
Give me the daggers. The sleeping and the dead
Are but as pictures. 'Tis the eye of childhood
That fears a painted devil. If he do bleed,
I'll **gild** the faces of the grooms withal,
For it must seem their guilt.

Exit. Knock within.

MACBETH   Whence is that knocking?
How is't with me, when every noise appals me?
What hands are here? Ha! They pluck out mine eyes.
Will all great Neptune's ocean wash this blood
Clean from my hand? No, **this my hand will rather**   60
The multitudinous seas incarnadine,
Making the green one red.

Enter Lady Macbeth.

L. MACBETH   My hands are of your colour; **but I shame**
To wear a heart so white. *(Knock within.)* I hear a
    knocking
At the south entry. Retire we to our chamber.
A little water clears us of this deed.
How easy is it then! **Your constancy**
Hath left you unattended. *(Knock within.)* Hark,
    more knocking.
Get on your nightgown, **lest occasion call us,**
And show us to be watchers. Be not lost   70
So poorly in your thoughts.

---

gild paint with gold.
this my hand . . . red my hand is more likely to turn the countless green seas blood-red.
but I shame . . . white but I am ashamed to have such a cowardly heart.
Your constancy . . . unattended Your firmness of purpose has deserted you.
lest occasion . . . watchers in case an occasion arises to call us and people realise we
have been up and awake.

MACBETH   To know my deed, 'twere best not know myself.

Knock within.

Wake Duncan with thy knocking. I would thou couldst.

Exeunt.

F4: The Dumb Waiter

Writer: Harold Pinter

Date: 1960

Staging: A set representing a basement room with two beds, flat against the back wall. Between the two beds is a serving hatch and a 'dumb waiter' – a lift which, in a café, can take food up to the dining room from the kitchen. To the left is a door which leads to the kitchen and lavatory. To the right is the door to the passage.

The story so far

Ben and Gus have arrived in a deserted basement flat. They appear to be hit-men waiting to do a job. After a series of mysterious happenings (an envelope containing matches is pushed under the door, the dumb waiter descends with an order for food . . .), Gus gets the jitters and Ben decides that it is time to repeat their instructions.

BEN   *(in a low voice)* Time's getting on.

GUS   I know. I don't like doing a job on an empty stomach.

BEN   *(wearily)* Be quiet a minute. Let me give you your instructions.

GUS   What for? We always do it the same way, don't we?

BEN   Let me give you your instructions.

> *Gus sighs and sits next to Ben on the bed. The instructions are stated and repeated automatically.*

When we get the call, you go over and stand behind the door.

GUS   Stand behind the door.

BEN   If there's a knock on the door you don't answer it.

GUS   If there's a knock on the door I don't answer it.   10

BEN   But there won't be a knock on the door.

GUS   So I won't answer it.

BEN	When the bloke comes in –
GUS	When the bloke comes in –
BEN	Shut the door behind him.
GUS	Shut the door behind him.
BEN	Without divulging your presence.
GUS	Without divulging my presence.
BEN	He'll see me and come towards me.
GUS	He'll see you and come towards you.	20
BEN	He won't see you.
GUS	*(absently)* Eh?
BEN	He won't see you.
GUS	He won't see me.
BEN	But he'll see me.
GUS	He'll see you.
BEN	He won't know you're there.
GUS	He won't know you're there.
BEN	He won't know *you're* there.
GUS	He won't know I'm there.	30
BEN	I take out my gun.
GUS	You take out your gun.
BEN	He stops in his tracks.
GUS	He stops in his tracks.
BEN	If he turns round –
GUS	If he turns round –
BEN	You're there.
GUS	I'm here.

Ben frowns and presses his forehead.

You've missed something out.

| BEN | I know. What? | 40 |

GUS   I haven't taken my gun out, according to you.

BEN   You take your gun out –

GUS   After I've closed the door.

BEN   After you've closed the door.

GUS   You've never missed that out before, you know that?

BEN   When he sees you behind him –

GUS   Me behind him –

BEN   And me in front of him –

GUS   And you in front of him –

BEN   He'll feel uncertain –   50

GUS   Uneasy.

BEN   He won't know what to do.

GUS   So what will he do?

BEN   He'll look at me and he'll look at you.

GUS   We won't say a word.

BEN   We'll look at him.

GUS   He won't say a word.

BEN   He'll look at us.

GUS   And we'll look at him.

BEN   Nobody says a word.   60

Pause.

GUS   What do we do if it's a girl?

BEN   We do the same.

GUS   Exactly the same?

BEN   Exactly.

Pause.

GUS   We don't do anything different?

BEN We do exactly the same.

GUS Oh.

Gus rises, and shivers.

Excuse me.

He exits through the door on the left. Ben remains sitting on the bed, still.

The lavatory chain is pulled once off left, but the lavatory does not flush.

Silence.

Gus re-enters and stops inside the door, deep in thought. He looks at Ben, then walks slowly across to his own bed. He is troubled. He stands, thinking. He turns and looks at Ben. He moves a few paces towards him.

(Slowly in a low, tense voice) Why did he send us matches if he knew there was no gas?

70

Silence.

Ben stares in front of him. Gus crosses to the left side of Ben, to the foot of his bed, to get to his other ear.

Ben. Why did he send us matches if he knew there was no gas?

Ben looks up.

Why did he do that?

BEN Who?

GUS Who sent us those matches?

BEN What are you talking about?

Gus stares down at him.

GUS *(thickly)* Who is it upstairs?

BEN	*(nervously)* What's one thing to do with another?
GUS	Who is it, though?
BEN	What's one thing to do with another?

80

Ben fumbles for his paper on the bed.

GUS	I asked you a question.
BEN	Enough!
GUS	*(with growing agitation)* I asked you before. Who moved in? I asked you. You said the people who had it before moved out. Well, who moved in?
BEN	*(hunched)* Shut up.
GUS	I told you, didn't I?
BEN	*(standing)* Shut up!
GUS	*(feverishly)* I told you before who owned this place, didn't I? I told you.

90

Ben hits him viciously on the shoulder.

I told you who ran this place, didn't I?

Ben hits him viciously on the shoulder.

(Violently) Well, what's he playing all these games for? That's what I want to know. What's he doing it for?

BEN	What games?
GUS	*(passionately, advancing)* What's he doing it for? We've been through our tests, haven't we? We got right through our tests, years ago, didn't we? We took them together, don't you remember, didn't we? We've proved ourselves before now, haven't we? We've always done our job. What's he doing all this for? What's the idea? What's he playing these games for?

100

The box in the shaft comes down behind them. The noise is this time accompanied by a shrill whistle, as it falls. Gus rushes to the hatch and seizes the note.

(Reading) Scampi!

He crumples the note, picks up the tube, takes out the whistle, blows and speaks.

WE'VE GOT NOTHING LEFT! NOTHING! DO YOU UNDERSTAND?

Ben seizes the tube and flings Gus away. He follows Gus and slaps him hard, back-handed, across the chest.

BEN   Stop it! You maniac!

GUS   But you heard!

BEN   *(savagely)* That's enough! I'm warning you!

Silence.

Ben hangs the tube. He goes to his bed and lies down. He picks up his paper and reads.

Silence.

The box goes up.

They turn quickly, their eyes meet. Ben turns to his paper.

Slowly Gus goes back to his bed, and sits.

Silence.

The hatch falls back into place.

They turn quickly, their eyes meet. Ben turns back to his paper.

Silence.

Ben throws his paper down.

BEN   Kaw!

He picks up the paper and looks at it.

Listen to this!

Pause.

What about that, eh?

Pause.

Kaw!

Pause.

Have you ever heard such a thing?   110

GUS   *(dully)* Go on!

BEN   It's true.

GUS   Get away.

BEN   It's down here in black and white.

GUS   *(very low)* Is that a fact?

BEN   Can you imagine it.

GUS   It's unbelievable.

BEN   It's enough to make you want to puke, isn't it?

GUS   *(almost inaudible)* Incredible.

*Ben shakes his head. He puts the paper down and rises. He fixes
the revolver in his holster.*

Gus stands up. He goes towards the door on the left.

BEN   Where are you going?   120

GUS   I'm going to have a glass of water.

*He exits. Ben brushes dust off his clothes and shoes. The whistle
in the speaking-tube blows. He goes to it, takes the whistle out
and puts the tube to his ear. He listens. He puts it to his mouth.*

BEN   Yes.

To ear. He listens. To mouth.

Straight away. Right.

To ear. He listens. To mouth.

Sure we're ready.

To ear. He listens. To mouth.

Understood. Repeat. He has arrived and will be coming in straight away. The normal method to be employed. Understood.

To ear. He listens. To mouth.

Sure we're ready.

To ear. He listens. To mouth.

Right.

He hangs the tube up.

Gus!   130

He takes out a comb and combs his hair, adjusts his jacket to diminish the bulge of the revolver. The lavatory flushes off left. Ben goes quickly to the door, left.

Gus!

The door right opens sharply. Ben turns, his revolver levelled at the door.

Gus stumbles in. He is stripped of his jacket, waistcoat, tie, holster and revolver.

He stops, body stooping, his arms at his sides. He raises his head and looks at Ben.

A long silence. They stare at each other.

Curtain

Activities: Section F, Mystery and Suspense

F1: Sherlock Holmes and the Limehouse Horror, page 194.

1   Perform the scene in groups of four, bringing out the differences
    between the evil Reichenbach, the terrified Sir Henry, the cringing
    'tramp' and the loyal Watson. Then discuss what makes your
    character's language and behaviour so distinctive.

2   Philip Pullman does not add stage directions to the characters'
    speeches, such as (*angrily*) or (*with a sudden movement*). Add
    some directions of this kind to the exchange between
    Reichenbach, the Tramp and Sir Henry (lines 35–60, from the point
    where Sir Henry spots the tramp to '. . . this is a human being.'), to
    help the actors understand how to deliver their speeches.

3   Write another scene involving these characters, for example
    when Holmes confronts Reichenbach. Make sure that the
    characters are clearly distinguished from each other by the
    way they talk and behave.

F2: The Woman in Black, page 201.

1   In pairs, make a recording of the second half of the extract, as
    though it were a radio play (from the point where Kipps begins to
    look through the papers – line 51). Produce sound effects for the
    scene in the graveyard (wind and waves on the shore?), the door
    slamming, the 'sound like an intermittent bump or rumble', which
    gets louder, the child's cry and 'the slightest of breezes'.

2   In pairs, discuss how the suspense is created in a stage
    performance through a combination of a) the dialogue itself;
    b) the sound effects; c) visual effects.

3   Re-read the extract, paying particular attention to Kipps's
    movements as they are described in the stage directions. List the
    different locations that have to be represented on stage. Now

sketch out a design for the set and write a brief explanation to go with it. There are a number of difficulties to resolve. How does the stage represent both the room in which Kipps is working and the graveyard (there is mention of a gauze)?

- Where does the actor go when he 'moves cautiously through the house'?
- How can you represent moonlight appearing and disappearing 'through the many windows'?
- Where is the door through which the strange sound comes?

F3: Waiting for Godot, page 207.

1   At the end of this section of dialogue, Estragon asks for some quiet and, during the silence that follows, he falls asleep. When Vladimir wakes him (because he feels lonely), Estragon says that he has been dreaming. In pairs, improvise some more lines of dialogue between the two tramps. Start with Vladimir waking Estragon.

2   Since *Waiting for Godot* was written in 1955, it has been performed by countless pairs of actors, and people have seen many different meanings in it. From your reading of this section, discuss the following questions in pairs:

- Who do you think Godot is?
- Why are they waiting for him?

What do you think are the differences between the two tramps? Which two television or film actors could you imagine as Vladimir and Estragon?

3   Write your own section of Vladimir–Estragon dialogue. You could base it on the improvisation you did in question 1.

F4: Macbeth, page 210.

1 There have been several film versions of *Macbeth*. Perform
   Macbeth's soliloquy from Scene 1 in pairs, with one of you reading
   the speech, like a 'voice-over', representing Macbeth's thoughts,
   and the other playing Macbeth and performing his actions, such as
   grasping for the dagger. Then swap roles. When you have done
   that, discuss two questions which face anyone making a film of
   this play:

   • Should the cinema audience see the dagger?
   • Should the soliloquy be in voice-over, or should the actor speak
     it out loud to himself?

   Now look back at the activity on iambic pentameter (pages 107–8).
   What do you notice about the way in which the verse is set out in
   Scene 2 line 17. Perform it in pairs and express the panic that the
   two characters are already experiencing.

2 Shakespeare has decided *not* to show us the scene with the
   grooms that Macbeth describes in Scene 2 or the actual murder
   of Duncan.

   • Write down what happens in the 'missing scene' in note form,
     from the point where Lady Macbeth enters Duncan's room to
     plant the daggers, up to Macbeth's murder of the King and his
     exit with the daggers still in his hand.
   • Discuss why it is important that we should imagine this scene
     vividly, but not actually see it acted out.

3 Write an account of this whole section of *Macbeth*, showing how
   the tension builds up through:

   • the language
   • Macbeth's account of the killing
   • the characters' actions (such as the point where Macbeth
     reveals that he has brought the daggers down with him).

F5: The Dumb Waiter, page 217.

1   In small groups, read (but don't act out) the sequence in which
    Ben takes Gus through the instructions, but only as far as 'I'm
    here' (lines 5–38). Give the impression that Ben is in charge and
    that Gus is a little nervous.

    - Now act out the series of instructions, this time with a third
      person playing the part of the unnamed victim.
    - Discuss why Gus is concerned that Ben has forgotten to remind
      him to take his gun out.

2   By the end of the play, Gus has become very jittery. In your groups,
    list the odd events which have built up the tension and
    contributed to Gus's unease. The first might be when Ben forgets
    to remind him about the gun.

3   Discuss what you think has happened at the end of the play, and
    what is about to happen. Then write a different ending which
    would fit everything that has led up to it.

Appendices

Ancient Greece	
600 BCE	**500 BCE**
	458 BCE *The Agamemnon*
525–Æschylus–456	
	480 ***Battle of Salamis***

Medieval England		
1200	**1300**	**1400**
Mystery plays	*Mystery plays*	*Mystery plays*
1215 ***Magna Carta***		1455–***Wars of the Roses***–1485

from Shakespeare to Wilde

1500	1600	1700	1800
Mystery plays c 1510 *Everyman*	1589–1606 *Doctor Faustus* *Romeo and Juliet Henry V* *Hamlet Twelfth Night* *Volpone*	1775 *The Rivals*	1895 *The Importance* *of Being Earnest*

1564–Christopher Marlow–1593
1564–William Shakespeare–1616
1572–Ben Jonson – 1637

1751–Richard Brinsley Sheridan–1816
1854–Oscar Wilde–1900
1856 G.B. Shaw born
1894 J.B. Priestley born
1896 R.C. Sherriff born

1588 ***The Armada*** 1605	***Gunpowder Plot***

The twentieth century up to the 1970s

1900	1950
1913 *Pygmalion* 1928 *Journey's End*	1946 *An Inspector Calls* 1955 *Waiting for Godot* 1960 *The Dumb Waiter* 1966 *Loot* 1972 *Sizwe Bansi Is Dead* 1975 *Faulty Towers 'The Builders'*

1906 – Samuel Beckett born

G.B. Shaw–died 1950   R.C. Sherriff–died 1975
1933–Joe Orton–1967

1914–18 ***The Great War***	1939–45 ***The Second World War***

Recent times
1980

1980 *I Will Marry When I Want*	1980 *Educating Rita*	1982 *Top Girls*	1985 *The Mysteries*	1985 *Sherlock Holmes and the Limehouse Horror*
	???? *The Revengers' Comedies*	1988 *Our Country's Good*		1992 *Maid Marian and Her Merry Men*
1991 *The Woman In Black*	1993 *The Odyssey*	1993 *Red Dwarf 'Marooned'*		1999 *Shakespeare In Love*
	1998 *Blackadder Goes Forth*			1999 *Ted Hughes's Tales From Ovid*

J.B. Priestley – died 1984	Samuel Beckett – died 1989
1991 ***end of apartheid***	

The dates of living playwrights have not been included.

From the National Curriculum (Key Stages 3–4)

This collection has been written to support the National Curriculum. The particular National Curriculum requirements which can be met through use of this collection are outlined below.

*At Key Stages 3 and 4, students are expected to participate in a wide variety of drama activities and be able to evaluate their own and others' contributions, such as (**En1, 4 Drama**):*

- improvising and working in role
- devising, scripting and performing in plays
- appreciating how the structure and organisation of scenes and plays contribute to dramatic effect
- evaluating critically performances of dramas that they have watched or in which they have taken part.

*They should learn (**En2, 2 English literary heritage**):*

- how and why texts have been influential and significant (or example, the influence of Greek myths, the Authorised Version of the Bible, the Arthurian legends).

*They should have the opportunity to read (**En2, 8 Literature**):*

- two plays by Shakespeare
- drama by major playwrights (such as: Congreve, Goldsmith, Marlowe, O'Casey, Pinter, Priestley, Shaffer, Shaw, Sheridan, Wilde)
- recent and contemporary drama written for young people and for adults (such as: Ayckbourn, Beckett, Bennett, Bolt, Friel, Willis Hall, Hare, Willy Russell, R.C.Sherriff, Wesker)
- drama by major writers from different cultures and traditions (such as: Athol Fugard, Arthur Miller, Wole Soyinka,Tennessee Williams).

*As part of their writing curriculum, students should (**En3, 1 Composition**):*

- draw on their experience of watching and performing in plays
- learn how to write in a range of forms, including playscripts
- use different ways to convey action, character, atmosphere and tension when they are scripting and performing plays (for example, through dialogue, movement and pace).

From the Framework for Teaching English

The following tables for years 7, 8 and 9 highlight the Framework objectives addressed in this collection.

Year 7	Sentence level work
	Standard English and language variation: 18. identify specific ways sentence structure and punctuation are different in older texts
	Text level work
	7. identify the main points, processes or ideas in a text and how they are sequenced and developed by the writer
	8. infer and deduce meanings using evidence in the text, identifying where and how meanings are implied
	Understanding the author's craft
	12. comment, using appropriate terminology, on how writers convey setting, character and mood through word choice and sentence structure
	14. recognise how writers' language choices can enhance meaning, e.g. *repetition, emotive vocabulary, varied sentence structure and line length, sound effects*
	15. trace the ways in which a writer structures a text to prepare a reader for the ending, and comment on the effectiveness of the ending
	Study of literary texts
	18. give a considered response to a play, as a script, on screen or in performance, focusing on interpretation of action, character and event
	20. explore the notion of literary heritage and understand why some texts have been particularly influential or significant
	Drama
	15. develop drama techniques to explore in role a variety of situations and texts or respond to stimuli
	16. work collaboratively to devise and present scripted and unscripted pieces which maintain the attention of an audience
	17. extend their spoken repertoire by experimenting with language in different roles and dramatic contexts
	19. reflect on and evaluate their own presentations and those of others

Year 8	Sentence level work
	Standard English and language variation:
	11. understand the differences between Standard English and dialectical variations
	13. recognise some of the differences in sentence structure, vocabulary and tone between a modern English text and a text from another historical period
	Text level work
	4. review their developing skills as active, critical readers who search for meaning using a range of reading strategies
	5. trace the development of themes, values or ideas in texts
	7. identify the ways implied and explicit meanings are conveyed in different texts
	Understanding the author's craft
	10. analyse the overall structure of a text to identify how key ideas are developed, e.g. *through the organization of content and the patterns of language used*
	11. investigate the different ways familiar themes are explored and presented by different writers
	Study of literary texts
	15. identify links between literary heritage texts and their times
	16. recognise how texts refer to and reflect the culture in which they were produced, e.g. *in their evocation of places and values*
	Drama
	13. reflect on their participation in drama and identify areas for their development of dramatic techniques
	14. develop the dramatic techniques that enable them to create and sustain a variety of roles
	15. explore and develop ideas, issues and relationships through role

Year 9	Sentence level work
	Standard English and language variation:
	11. investigate ways English has changed over time and identify current trends of language change, e.g. *word meanings*
	Text level work
	6. comment on the authorial perspectives offered in texts on individuals, community and society in texts from different cultures
	7. compare the presentation of ideas, values or emotions in related or contrasting texts
	9. compare themes and styles of two writers from different times
	Study of literary texts
	14. analyse the language, form and dramatic impact of scenes and plays by published dramatists
	15. extend their understanding of literary heritage by relating major writers to their historical context, and explaining their appeal over time
	Drama
	12. use a range of drama techniques, including work in role, to explore issues, ideas and meanings
	13. develop and compare different interpretations of scenes or plays by Shakespeare or other dramatists
	15. write critical evaluations of performances they have seen or in which they have participated, identifying the contributions of the writer, director and actors

PLAYWRIGHT	PLAY	SCENE
Comedy of situation		
Tony Robinson, C.20-21	*Maid Marian and her Merry Men*	In the stocks
Ayckbourn, C.20-21	*The Revengers' Comedies*	Henry saves Karen – and himself
Shakespeare, C.16-17	*Twelfth Night*	Malvolio appears in yellow stockings

PLAYWRIGHT	PLAY	SCENE
Comedy and deception		
Grant & Naylor, C.20-21	*Red Dwarf*	Lister behaves selflessly
Joe Orton, C.20	*Loot*	The money and the coffin
anon, C.13 (Tony Harrison's version)	*Mak the sheep-stealer*	Mak disguises a sheep as a baby

PLAYWRIGHT	PLAY	SCENE
Comedy of words		
Marc Norman & Tom Stoppard, C.20-21	*Shakespeare in Love*	Henslowe gets out of a hot spot
Willy Russell, C.20-21	*Educating Rita*	Rita and *Macbeth*
Oscar Wilde, C.19	*The Importance of Being Earnest*	Jack answers Lady Bracknell

PLAYWRIGHT	PLAY	SCENE
Comedy and the English language		
Connie Booth & John Cleese, C.20-21	*Fawlty Towers*	Manuel takes charge
G. B. Shaw, C.20	*Pygmalion*	'Done her in'
Sheridan, C.18	*The Rivals*	Jack deceives Mrs Malaprop

PLAYWRIGHT	PLAY	SCENE
History		
Timberlake Wertenbaker, C.20-21	*Our Country's Good*	Bound for Sydney Cove

PLAYWRIGHT	PLAY	SCENE
History and war		
R. C. Sherriff, early C.20	*Journey's End*	Going 'over the top'
Curtis & Elton C.20-21	*Blackadder Goes Forth*	The final scenes
Shakespeare, C.16-17	*Henry V*	Henry rallies the troops

PLAYWRIGHT	PLAY	SCENE
Tragedy		
Æschylus, C.4 BCE	*The Agamemnon*	Agamemnon kills his daughter
Shakespeare, C.16-17	*Romeo and Juliet*	The Friar's letter is not delivered

PLAYWRIGHT	PLAY	SCENE
Marlowe, C.16	*Doctor Faustus*	Faustus sells his soul to Mephistophilis
Shakespeare, C.16-17	*Hamlet*	The ghost demands revenge

Viewpoints on society		
J. B. Priestley, mid C.20	*An Inspector Calls*	Mr Birling states his case
Ngugi wa Thiongo & Ngugi wa Mirii, C.20-21	*I Will Marry When I Want*	A modern daughter
Athol Fugard, John Kani, Winston Ntshona, C.20-21	*Sizwe Bansi Is Dead*	Sizwe changes his identity
Caryl Churchill, C.20-21	*Top Girls*	Griselda tells her story
Ben Jonson, C.17	*Volpone*	The cheating of Corvino

PLAYWRIGHT	PLAY	SCENE
Myth and morality		
anon, C.15	*Everyman*	Death visits Everyman
Derek Walcott, C.20-21	*The Odyssey*	After the funeral of Achilles
Ted Hughes C.20	*Tales from Ovid*	Apollo gives Midas ass's ears

PLAYWRIGHT	PLAY	SCENE
Mystery and suspense		
Philip Pullman, C.20-21	*Sherlock Holmes and The Limehouse Horror*	Confrontation with the giant rat
Stephen Ma latratt, C.20-21	*The Woman in Black*	Strange noises
Samuel Beckett, C.20	*Waiting for Godot*	'He should be here.'
Shakespeare, C.16-17	*Macbeth*	Murdering a king
Harold Pinter, C.20-21	*The Dumb Waiter*	Waiting for the victim to enter